Life
Lessons
From Alpha
to Omega

Life Lessons

From Alpha to Omega

Richard H. Schmidt

June 26, 2005

To Sarah,
with every good wish, and
may God bless you.

Richard H. Schmidt

SEABURY BOOKS
an imprint of
CHURCH PUBLISHING, NEW YORK

A catalog record for this book is available from
the Library of Congress

ISBN 1-59627-012-8

Church Publishing Incorporated
445 Fifth Avenue
New York, NY 10016
www.churchpublishing.org

5 4 3 2 1

To Pam,
my one and only sweetheart.
I love you too.

Contents

Preface

Some things can't be taught in school. They must be learned through experience, trial and error, hard knocks. This book contains the lessons I didn't learn in school. Why I didn't learn them there doesn't matter, but if I had, it would have made for smoother sailing later on.

Vignettes and people fill the pages of this book. Every experience related in these pages actually happened to me, and every person mentioned is someone I actually know or have known. Each experience and each person taught me something.

Because I have spent most of my life as a Christian pastor, the context of most of these vignettes is the parish church. The settings are vestry meetings, nursing homes, monasteries, parishioners' homes, the pastor's study, and other places frequented by the clergy. Moreover, because it is my nature to ruminate about spiritual matters, many of the things I learned pertain to spirituality. But this book is not primarily about church. It is about life, spiritual and otherwise. The experiences related in these pages are common to most people — learning what matters and what doesn't, listening between the lines to what people say, balancing family and professional obligations, dealing with institutions, authority figures, clients (parishioners), ego and ambition, self-doubt, controversy, wanting to belong, and hopes and dreams. I expect the clergy deal with these life issues pretty much as everyone else does, usually by the seat of our pants. I believe I would have learned many of the same things had I been an attorney, businessperson, or salesclerk, and I hope the insights contained in these pages will be useful to people in all callings and circumstances.

The lessons learned in my thirty years as a priest are interwoven with the places where I served and the people I came to know there. These pages will therefore make more sense to the reader if I begin with a brief outline of my career as a clergyman.

In May 1970, I graduated from Vanderbilt Divinity School in Nashville, Tennessee, with a master of divinity degree. That's the degree leading to parish ministry in the Episcopal Church and many other denominations.

A month after graduating from Vanderbilt, I was ordained, and my wife, Pam, and I moved to Romney, West Virginia. We had been married two years and Pam was six months pregnant at the time. Romney is a small town on the South Branch of the Potomac River, a gently flowing stream ideal for tubing and fishing, and far removed, both geographically and politically, from the city most people associate with the Potomac. The mountains around Romney were clothed in apple, peach, and pear orchards. I had been named deacon-in-charge (later vicar) of St. Stephen's Episcopal Church in Romney and Emmanuel Episcopal Church in Moorefield, another small town twenty-eight miles away. I conducted a Sunday service in each church, with an average attendance of about two dozen in Romney and half a dozen or so in Moorefield. It took me about three weeks to learn the names of everyone in both congregations.

In October 1971, I accepted an offer to move to St. John's Episcopal Church in Charleston, West Virginia. St. John's was a vigorous downtown parish a few blocks from the state capitol, the largest parish in the diocese at that time. It had programs and ministries I had only dreamt about in Romney. I was the third priest on the staff and by far the youngest and least experienced. I shared equally in the preaching and liturgical ministries and was charged specifically with the oversight of youth programs. My four years at St. John's included two as assistant rector, then a year as the acting rector while the parish sought a new rector, and a year under the clergyman called to that position.

Eager for a parish of my own, I was pleased to be called in 1975 to serve as rector of Christ Episcopal Church in Fairmont, West Virginia. Fairmont had been a prosperous coal mining town some years earlier, but by 1975, many of the mines and related industries had closed and the town had begun to lose population as people relocated to find work. The once-vibrant downtown area consisted largely of government offices and empty storefronts. We used to say, "The last one out of Fairmont, please turn out the lights." Christ Church, like the town, had seen more prosperous times. Of the four hundred or so names on the roll, we had only one parishioner whom I would have called wealthy. Everyone else struggled to make ends meet, as did the congregation itself. The people were down-to-earth, unpretentious, and as solid as the mountains. Pam and I look upon our seven years in Fairmont as among the happiest of our lives.

When I was called in 1982 to become rector of St. Peter's Episcopal Church in Ladue, Missouri, a suburb of St. Louis, I knew it would be different. The church was several times larger than Christ Church, Fairmont, and the Ladue zip code had ranked as the nation's sixth wealthiest in the 1980 census. Large homes set back from the road by expansive yards were the norm. Many parishioners' children attended private schools in the area, but the Ladue public schools were also top-rate. St. Peter's worshiped in a splendid Georgian colonial church. Opportunities for musical and liturgical ministries abounded. St. Peter's taught me more than any other parish I served, both because the challenges were greater and because of the broad array of skills, knowledge, and experiences my St. Peter's parishioners possessed. I like to think they learned a little from me, but I know I learned a lot from them.

I received a telephone call from out of the blue in February 1988. Would I consider leaving my position at St. Peter's and moving to Philadelphia to become editor of *The Episcopalian,* a national monthly newspaper with 250,000 subscribers? I had done some newspaper work over the years, and editing *The Episcopalian* had long been a dream of mine. I was ready to try something different, so I accepted the position. I loved the work, but church politics and finances meant that *The Episcopalian*'s days were numbered, and two years later I was looking for a new job.

If someone had told me in 1990 that Pam and I would find happiness in a small town in south Alabama, I would have laughed. But Alabama had the last laugh — or perhaps God did. We took our family, now three nearly grown sons, to live in Daphne, Alabama, where I became rector of St. Paul's Episcopal Church. Daphne was a growing bedroom community seven miles across Mobile Bay from the city of Mobile, Alabama. A series of personnel problems had caused several difficult years at St. Paul's, but parishioners seemed eager to put that behind them — and they did. During my time there, the congregation tripled in size and we built a new church, doubling the seating capacity, to accommodate the new people. Pam and I felt completely at home among the people of St. Paul's, and nowhere did I feel so appreciated as I felt there.

After ten years in Daphne, I realized the parish needed a leader with new ideas and I needed a fresh challenge. Pam and I decided that, after thirty years in parish ministry, I would take early retirement. Since then, I have written three books and taught Anglican spirituality in Nigeria and in England. I now serve two days a week at Grace Church in Kirkwood, Missouri, and the future appears to hold a variety of appealing challenges.

As a young man, I told myself I could endure nearly anything so long as I was still growing and learning. To date, I have not been disappointed. Each place where Pam and I have lived and all the people we have known have taught us valuable lessons, pushed us to expand our vision, challenged us to grow. That's what this book is about. If a reader of these pages learns from them something that I failed to learn in school and had to learn by more difficult means later, this book will have served its purpose.

I express my appreciation to those who read the first draft of this manuscript, found errors I had missed, and suggested improvements of many kinds, most of which I have incorporated into this book. They include my wife, Pam, always my greatest fan and my most honest critic; my editor at Church Publishing, Joan Castagnone; my good friend and fellow priest Howard Park of Chesterfield, Missouri; my former warden and confidant, Stan Pylipow, also of Chesterfield, Missouri; my cousin Havard Bauer of Mt. Angel, Oregon; and David Pratt, a novelist and friend from Kingston, Ontario.

THE REV. DR. RICHARD H. SCHMIDT
Chesterfield, Missouri

Life
Lessons
From Alpha
to Omega

Aging

I've always wanted a wrinkled face, gnarled hands, and hunching shoulders. Most people can't imagine why. That's because they didn't enjoy my childhood.

My parents had grown up in the 1930s on West Main Street in Shelbyville, Kentucky, thirty miles east of Louisville. In those days Shelbyville was a sleepy county seat and tobacco market town of three thousand inhabitants. As children my parents had lived across the street from each other and been best friends for most of their lives. When my father was about to be deployed as a naval officer during the Second World War and realized he might never again see Shelbyville or the girl across the street, he suddenly knew he'd always wanted to marry her. He proposed to my mother on Christmas Eve, 1943. They were married seven days later, on New Year's Eve, and my father left for the war a week after that. I was born on September 26, 1944.

The war ended and my father returned to Shelbyville, my mother, and me. When another son and a daughter were born to them, his parents vacated their large, rambling house so that we could move in. They built another house on the lot next door. My mother's parents still lived across the street. As a result, my brother and sister and I had three homes, and often those of our grandparents were our favorites, because they read us stories, taught us to grow flowers in the garden, took us for rides in the country, and cooked our favorite dishes whenever we wanted them — even when they weren't good for us. And that's not all of it. On adjacent and kitty-cornered lots lived half a dozen or so great aunts, uncles, and cousins, from both sides of my family. They treated us as indulgently as our grandparents did.

As a youngster, I took my large and loving extended family for granted. I thought everyone grew up that way. Those elderly kinfolk have been a blessing to me through the years (though not an unmixed one — when as an adolescent I sought to put some distance between myself and my family, it was hard to find anywhere to go). Part of that blessing is the feelings I've always had about growing old, something I learned from my relatives at an early age. Wrinkled faces, gnarled hands, and hunching shoulders suggested warmth, wisdom, and grace to me when I was a youngster. I wanted to be like those people when I grew up. I still do.

I recently overheard someone say to an eighty-year-old, "You look wonderful, not a day over sixty!" Perhaps the remark was meant as a compliment, but I heard it as prejudicial, almost like saying to an African American, "You are so articulate that you sound white," or to a woman, "You're so talented that I'd have thought you were a man." Not long ago I was stunned by a television commercial in which a father and his teenage daughter were discussing the new car he was buying for her. Pointing to the car being advertised, the daughter said, "I want that one, not one that will make me look old and stupid." She and her father then laughed, as if equating old with stupid were beyond question. Prejudice against the aged is so pervasive in our society that we don't recognize it. Who says it is better to look young than old? By what canon is taut skin prettier than wrinkled skin? Why do Americans spend billions of dollars each year on cosmetics and clothing — and why do some people take up with a lover half their age — merely to perpetuate the fiction that we do not grow old?

Youth is more agreeable than old age in some ways, but old age is more agreeable in others, and neither is inherently good or bad.

Thoughts and behaviors are good or bad, but age is not. In some Asian societies, the prevailing view is just the opposite of ours: people strive to look older than they are because age brings respect and honor. The best English translation of the word for "elderly" in the Yoruba language of Nigeria is "wisdom people." That's the way I've always seen it; what the years take away in energy, they give back in wisdom. I've known that for as long as I can remember. If asked as a youngster to name the best age to be, I'd have said seventy-five. Very early in life I learned to see people who had attained that age as free simply to be, with no need to produce or achieve anything.

I once heard someone say that life is like a single trip around the face of a clock. For the first six hours, from 12:00 until 6:00, we take on things — academic degrees, dreams, relationships, responsibilities. Then for the last six hours, we let go of things, including resentments and unrealistic expectations. As we approach 12:00 again, we lighten our load and discover wisdom, acceptance, wonder, gratitude, forgiveness, and simplicity, things we hadn't made time for earlier. That has already begun to happen for me, and if I am granted the time and remain open to the grace of God, I hope old age will bring more and more of it to me.

I don't mean to discount the suffering that is often a part of aging. My eighty-five-year-old mother recently commented to me that growing old is "not for sissies." She knows what she's talking about. My mother can barely breathe because her rib cage is collapsing onto her lungs. I also remember my paternal grandmother's death just five years ago, at the age of 101, ten years after her mind had given up. And in my role as a pastor I've visited countless elderly people and observed the hardships they face. Aging is especially burdensome for the poor who cannot afford the small comforts and ameliorations available to others. In time I know that, barring a sudden death, my own faculties will wane, and I will begin to experience the frailties and pains that today I have only observed in others. They are part of growing old, and I don't look forward to them. I also know, however, that people deal differently with aging, and how I deal with it will be my decision.

I shall never forget a visit I made to a nursing home in Alabama. I saw two women residents, both in their nineties and both in failing health. The first complained of everything. The nurses were surly and didn't answer her pages. The food was bland and cold. Her room was stuffy. No one visited her. Her doctor didn't listen to her. Her glasses were of the wrong prescription. Television bored her. And of course there were her various aches. The other resident, in virtually identical circumstances, could not have sounded happier. Her nurses looked in on her regularly. They brought her three meals a day and adjusted the thermostat and ventilation in her room. Friends telephoned from time to time, and the parish newsletter helped her keep up with things. Her doctor was busy but attentive. Television was such a blessing; she wondered how elderly people ever managed without it. As for her aches, I suppose she had them, but she declined to discuss them. The difference between the two women may have been partly inborn or learned, but I know part of it was a decision. No one likes infirmity, but happiness is a choice, and some of the happiest people I've known have been those who seemed to have the least reason to be happy. If I live long enough to experience the infirmity of old age, I hope I shall have the grace to choose happiness. Those who do so bring a blessing both to themselves and to those near to them.

Part of being happy in old age (or at any other time) is how we envision ourselves. Some elderly people see only their increasingly dysfunctional and cumbersome bodies. "I am an invalid" or "I am of no use to anyone," they repeat to themselves. I once visited a woman in a nursing home who, I assumed, would have such thoughts. But her sense of herself was so unexpectedly positive that it stunned me. I had not known her before. An attendant wheeled her into the room where I was to conduct a worship service. She was paralyzed from the waist down. As the other residents were gathering, I engaged her in conversation. "Tell me something about yourself," I said. "I'm a tennis player," she proclaimed. I marveled at her — paralyzed, in a wheelchair, and a tennis player! In her own mind, she was still the vibrant athlete dashing across the court to return a serve. She had not allowed her infirmity to define her identity, and though frail and in pain, she was radiant. It was a choice.

And it is a choice I hope to make for the rest of my life. For now — and I am one month shy of my sixtieth birthday as I write these words — it's an easy choice, because I enjoy life as I've never enjoyed it before. I am doing all the things I've dreamt of doing for the better part of six decades. But I am also beginning to look and sometimes to feel like an old man — sockets around my eyes, thinning white hair, occasional sleepless nights — and I know that is just the beginning. The future will probably call for courage, patience, acceptance, and good humor. I pray that I shall have those things when I need them. But with the slowing down of my body, I am also finding time to be myself, to listen to entire symphonies at a single sitting, to pray in an unhurried manner, and to be with the people I most enjoy. This is a gift that comes with aging. God has always been good to me, but I hope that growing old will be the best of all.

 **Anger**

"You bastards! First you take my job away, turn me out on the street. Then in the next breath you give me a standing ovation and tell me how grateful you are for the great job I've done. That was insensitive, two-faced, and cruel. If you were going to cut me down, why didn't you just do it and let me deal with what you'd done? Why did you try to make it so pleasant when there wasn't anything pleasant about it? Did the Nazis tell the Jews at Buchenwald how grateful they were for the Jews' contribution to German life? I'm sure they didn't. But they were at least honest about what they were doing, which is more than I can say for you.

"And God, as for you, you let this happen. You always let crummy things happen. What's the use of having a God who lets crummy things happen all the time?"

You correctly guessed that I was angry when I wrote those words, probably unreasonably angry (I do not normally liken church officials to Nazis). That was some years ago now. I had never lost a job before, but I was no stranger to anger.

Early in my career as a pastor, I had sometimes become angry at parishioners over insignificant little things. In particular, I was angry at nominal church members, those who would show up at church on Christmas and Easter, if then. Too polite (or scared) to voice my feelings aloud, I would mutter angry words under my breath:

"How dare you expect so much from me for your daughter's wedding when neither you nor your daughter ever darkens the church door on other occasions!"

"How dare you carry on here in the checkout line as if we were best buddies when you have hardly given me the opportunity to learn your name!"

"How dare you ask me to bring you communion privately now that you are in the hospital when you never availed yourself of it publicly when you were well!"

"How dare you give such a paltry sum when you have far more money than others who give ten times that amount!"

"How dare you ask me to baptize your baby when you show so little evidence of fulfilling your own baptismal vows!"

"How dare you not take the church as seriously as I do!"

Constant repetition of these "how dares" fuels resentment and bitterness. Perhaps the people with whom I was angry did have their priorities wrong and were in real spiritual danger. I don't know. But there could have been no doubt about me. Anyone who expends that much energy on anger is in very hot water.

Over the years, I have learned several things about anger:

The source of anger is often my injured pride. This is usually disguised as righteous indignation. I used to fancy myself a martyr, a role I felt became me. But as long as this attitude persisted, I could not reach out to others with the love of Christ because that love was not in me. When I am preoccupied with my own prerogatives and virtue, there's no room in my heart for other people, let alone God. I care only about myself.

My point of view, like all human points of view, is limited. I don't have all the information. I have neither the right nor the ability to peer into another person's soul and pass judgment on what I see there. How can I know the battles other people have fought, or, if I had been required to fight the same battles, whether I would have fared as well?

The only life I am called upon to run is my own. Other people, the parish, the diocese, the national church — these are not pieces on my chess board for me to move at will. I would do well to let others tend to whatever obstacles obstruct their way while I do some soul-searching of my own. Although in my anger I had been faithful in outward ways, the bitterness and resentment I had allowed into my soul threatened to turn me into a whitewashed tomb.

I need to keep looking at Jesus. That means I need *not* to be looking at church organizations, other people, or myself. Jesus is the standard against whom I am to measure my own life. He holds wide his arms to welcome both the wayward pastor and the wayward parishioner. If we are to move beyond our anger over the foolishness, mistakes, and duplicity of others, it will happen only when we attune our will to the will of Christ. Whether we are better or wiser than someone else doesn't matter. What matters is that we embrace one another as Christ embraces us all. The identities of some of those included might surprise us. And who knows? The fact that Christ includes us in his embrace may surprise some of them.

My anger at losing my job proved short-lived. One reason was that although it felt personal at the time, I soon realized it had more to do with church politics than with me. But the main reason my anger dissipated quickly was that when I found another job, it turned out to be the beginning of the happiest time in my life. Had I known that would happen, I suppose I wouldn't have gotten angry in the first place. How many times, I wonder, have I gotten angry when, had I really trusted God, I'd have known there was nothing to be angry about?

Born Again

> But he who would be born again indeed,
> Must wake his soul unnumbered times a day,
> And urge himself to life with holy greed;
> Now ope his bosom to the wind's free play;
> And now, with patience forceful, hard, lie still,
> Submiss and ready to the making will,
> Athirst and empty, for God's breath to fill.

—George Macdonald, in *Diary of an Old Soul*

Having grown up in a small Southern town where half the population belonged to the First Baptist Church, I am no stranger to the born-again question. Whether one was a "born-again Christian" was *the* religious question among many of my schoolmates, although it was rarely asked in the Presbyterian church where my family worshiped. Episcopalians don't usually ask the born-again question, either, but it's still in the air, particularly in the South, and I've been asked it now and then throughout my life. It behooves one to have an answer ready, especially if one is a preacher, and if at all possible, the answer should be yes.

But what is a "born-again Christian"? Many of my friends in high school could name the day and the hour they had become one, so I assumed born-again-ness was a sudden thing, a kind of spiritual lightning bolt. Certainly you'd recognize it when it happened to you, and certainly you'd remember it. But I couldn't say whether it had happened to me. I didn't think much about it, either as a schoolboy or as an adult, but the question made me uncomfortable when someone posed it. Now I think I have an answer, thanks in part to George Macdonald's little verse: I'm definitely born again. In fact, I've been born again, and again, and again, six times that I know of, and maybe a few times I've forgotten about or didn't notice.

My first born-again experience took place at 11:40 a.m., Sunday, April 4, 1948. That's when I was baptized at the First Presbyterian Church in Shelbyville, Kentucky, at the age of three. The next time was at a Billy Graham Crusade in Louisville, when I was twelve. It was there that I first knowingly gave my life to Christ. Then there was the day I married Pam, through whom I have learned more of the goodness and grace of God than from all the theological books I've ever read. Then came the day I entered alcoholism recovery, at the age of thirty-eight, and then the time I resigned as rector of a big and prestigious parish to take a big pay cut and go off to do something I had always dreamt of doing. And finally, there was the day, that dream now behind me, that I declined a move to another big, prestigious parish and chose instead a small parish in what everyone I knew regarded as the boonies. Each of these moments was a fresh beginning for me, building on the past to be sure, but also opening my soul to new glimpses of God's goodness and grace. After each of these moments, I was a changed man — I had been born again.

I hope to be born yet again, and again — even "unnumbered times a day," if it be God's will. This is a sort of "holy greed," I suppose, a longing for more and more of God. Having glimpsed God and grown familiar with the outskirts of his ways, I want more. "My soul is athirst for God, athirst for the living God," as the psalmist said. I have the sense that God has granted me a few sweet (and a few not so sweet) drafts of the water of life, but the full slaking of this thirst awaits me and will be given, sip by sip most likely, as I continue to grow in faithfulness.

Faithfulness can mean different things. Sometimes it means opening our bosom "to the wind's free play," a willingness to allow God to whisk us off to realms undreamt of. Faithfulness is ever open to the new, the unexpected, the perplexing. Faithfulness is always seeking. It is free; it moves around. If what we call faithfulness is pinched, narrow, or confined, it is something else. At other times, though, to be faithful means "with patience forceful, hard [to] lie still." This isn't easy, which is why patience must be "forceful, hard." Often the faithful act is simply to wait, to do nothing, and to trust that God will do what God will do when God will do it. If we are always striving to convince others to agree with us or to do our bidding, we do not act faithfully. That is pride, lusting for control. God is not calling us to prevail. Rather, it is God who will prevail, and we are often called to a humble, trustful waiting, "submiss and ready to the making will."

When we reach that point, the point of true and complete faithfulness, then I suppose we shall need no more rebirthings, for our souls will have drunk their fill and been made ready at last "for God's breath to fill." It is as in the words of the old song: "Spirit of the living God, fall afresh on me. Break me, melt me, mold me, fill me. Spirit of the living God, fall afresh on me."

$\mathcal{C}$ _____ Call

When I decided in 1968 that I wanted to be an Episcopal priest, I drove to Cincinnati to see Roger Blanchard, the bishop of the diocese where I resided at the time. He sent me off to see a psychiatrist. That's standard procedure, I later learned; some people want to be ordained for kooky reasons. The only thing I remember about my interview with the psychiatrist is what I said when he asked why I felt called to the priesthood. "I'm not sure I am called to the priesthood," I nervously admitted. "I'm not sure what a call is. I have heard no voices, seen no visions. But I love the church, its music and liturgy, and I love, or at least like, most of the people I meet in church. I think I am a good public speaker, and I enjoy working with people. I guess you could say I like the job description, if I understand it. And I love Jesus, or think I do, or try to, most of the time, anyway. Is that a call?" That answer was apparently agreeable to the psychiatrist, because the Diocese of Southern Ohio accepted me as a postulant for holy orders a short while later.

I'm still not sure what a call is. People speak of a call to ordained ministry. The clergy have a unique function in the church — but so do choristers, janitors, and youth group advisors. Doesn't God call them, too? And what about those who serve God in the secular world? Aren't those people called to ministry?

The church speaks of call in another sense as well. When a priest moves from one parish to another, she is not offered a position but is *called* to one. So far as I know, only in the church do people talk this way. Lawyers, beauticians, computer programmers, and short-order cooks do not speak of being called, but of choosing a career or getting a job, which amounts to the same thing so far as I can see. The whole call terminology sounds affected to me. My friend David Pratt, in an unpublished novel, has one of his characters, an English priest, say, "It's not a vocation, just a human decision. I don't like the idea of vocation [from the Latin *vocare*, to call]. I don't believe in holding God responsible for decisions we make. Like the Arabs say, take what you want, and pay for it. The price, in my case, is never being absolutely sure it was the right decision."

Upon moving to a new position, pastors like to say they're "answering a call." If a pastor is "called" to a parish, who does the calling? Is it the vestry of the parish issuing the call, or God? Many clergy speak as if it's God who calls them to a position. I've heard more than one priest, upon learning that he'd been nominated for bishop, say, "I'm leaving it in God's hands." The implication is that God determines the outcome of episcopal elections. But a few years later, I sometimes wonder. The relationship between priest and congregation, or bishop and diocese, occasionally turns out to be an unhappy one. Do we blame God for that? God is surely involved in the call process — I believe God is involved in everything — but I cannot believe God is solely responsible for the decisions human beings make. In my own case, the move to which I felt most clearly "called" was the one that turned out worst for me. Was that God's fault? If it was a mismatch, did God do it? I think not. So if it wasn't God's voice I heard calling in my ear when I agreed to go there, whose voice was it?

A call to a parish usually comes at the end of a long process of screening and interviewing. I have interviewed with at least three dozen search committees in my thirty years as a priest. A priest talks to search committees only when he is willing, or eager, to relocate.

Sometimes it's because the priest is unhappy where he is, but in my case, it was usually because I wanted a new challenge and felt I had done what I could do in my current parish and that it needed a new leader with a new vision. I loved being interviewed because I was the center of attention. I find sitting among people who lean forward in their chairs and listen intently to every word I utter a most gratifying way to spend an evening.

But most of these search processes left me disappointed in the end. For every call I received, I interviewed for several I did not receive. Usually I liked the people I had met and was excited about moving to their community. I was pumped up. The call process felt like a contest with winners and losers, though no one used those terms. When I received a "Dear John" letter in the mail, informing me that someone else was the lucky winner, it was as if I'd been punctured, like a balloon. The letters never included any explanation of what the winner had that I lacked. Upon learning that I was not called, I felt like a coat on a department store rack which an attractive customer had tried on and examined, only to hang me back on the rack and walk away, with no explanation of why I was not wanted.

Only once was I desperate to get out of a situation. I had begun to feel imprisoned where I was. For many sleepless nights I had tried to discern God's will for me, praying the plaintive psalms and writing long journal entries at 3:00 a.m., probing, searching, pleading with God. One such entry read, "Just tell me what you want me to do — *just tell me!* If you want me to remain here, I am willing to remain, despite my heavy heart when I think of this place. Maybe there are things here you want me to learn. Or if you want me to update my resume and seek another parish, I will do that. I've been told I'm unfit for parish ministry, so I will leave parish ministry if you want me to. I will do what you ask, Lord. *Just tell me!*" No answer came. Finally I went off to a monastery for a week to discern God's will for my life. Still, no answer came. Then, in my last hour at the monastery, just before I was to leave for the airport, I heard a voice in the back of my head saying,

"You certainly do take yourself seriously, Dick. Why don't you just relax and do what you're supposed to do? Return to your parish, and if you're still rector there tomorrow, do what the rector is supposed to do. If you're still rector there the next day, do what the rector is supposed to do again. I'm not calling you to *do* anything in particular. I don't care what kind of work you choose or where you live. My will is that whatever you do and wherever you are, you will love and enjoy me as I love and enjoy you. Whether to move is tomorrow's concern. Tend to today. You want to be obedient? Then stop demanding answers to tomorrow's questions. You don't need answers. When you need answers, I'll give you answers. Meanwhile, go back, do your job, relax, and quit your bellyaching."

I think that was a call.

$\mathcal{C}$ _____ **Conflict**

Wherever people gather, there will be politics, and wherever there is politics, there will be fights. The church is not immune, and those who expect to find it a placid oasis in an otherwise fractious world will soon become disillusioned. The people in church on Sunday are the same people found in the world the other six days of the week, and they don't check their weekday characters at the church door. Neither do the clergy.

In thirty years of parish ministry, I've been involved in my share of church fights. Here is a short list of the issues those fights appeared to be about: Should the Head Start program be allowed to meet in the parish hall during the week? Should the choirmaster be fired? Should a drug rehabilitation agency be given space in the church basement? Should the Unification Church be allowed to hold a worship service in the church? Should an ecumenical soup kitchen take place at the church or off the premises? Should the altar be relocated? Should the new Prayer Book be introduced? Should the details of my compensation package be made public? With limited money, what should be funded? Should an additional Sunday service be scheduled? Should Sunday school take place during the principal church service or before it? Should the main event on Christmas Eve be a children's pageant or the Holy Eucharist? Should guitar music be part of Sunday morning worship? Should gay people be given leadership positions in the parish? Should we build a new church or expand the old one? Should the parish take part in the diocesan capital funds drive when it was planning a capital funds drive of its own? Should a group of Buddhists be allowed to hold a worship service in the church?

I said that's what the fights *appeared* to be about, and at one level, they were. But underneath, all church fights are about the same thing. Whatever the issue may appear to be, church fights are all about who's in charge. It's a question of control. Always.

If you know the fight is really about control, you will fight more effectively — and more faithfully. I won some of the fights and lost some. Some became bitterly personal and caused me (and others) sleepless nights, but some hardly seemed like fights at all because the question was resolved so quickly and amicably.

Attendance at St. Peter's, Ladue, had begun to increase in the 1980s. The increase had been slow, but noticeable. I knew that when average attendance at a church's principal worship service reaches 75 percent of seating capacity, people feel crowded and growth stops. Newcomers will be discouraged, or if more new people begin attending, old-timers will stay away. If attendance is to continue growing, a change is needed. This could mean enlarging the church, founding a new congregation, or adding a worship service. I proposed adding a third Sunday morning service.

Enlarging the church was unthinkable because St. Peter's was an architectural gem. I felt more time was needed before the parish could be excited about founding a new congregation. That left adding a worship service. Children had been excluded from worship at St. Peter's, and I saw this not only as a way to ease crowding, but as an opportunity to bring children into corporate worship. I announced to the congregation at the annual parish meeting that we would institute a third Sunday service the following month, designed specifically for families with young children. I used a restaurant analogy to explain the change, saying that it would be like adding a new line of food to the menu. "A restaurant that serves nothing but hamburgers may do a good business, but if it adds a salad bar or a line of seafood dishes, business will pick up," I said.

Over a hundred people attended the first nine o'clock family service. That was not a full church, but it was a viable number. I was encouraged. Total attendance at three services was significantly greater than total attendance had been at two. But the nine o'clock attendance stopped growing. Within six months, it had dropped to an average of fewer than thirty — not a viable number. I had to admit that my idea had not taken root. We dropped the family service.

I now see that I was part of the problem. At first, I had been acting solely on principle, but before long, it had become a matter of control. My principles were, I still believe, correct — meet a challenge before it becomes a problem; provide a variety of worship experiences; make children an important part of worship. Principles are important, and we should take them seriously, but principles can become mixed up with our unacknowledged control needs. We can run over people while charging ahead, our principles held high. This is not only poor leadership; it's lousy Christianity, and it can cause a fight that becomes personal and bloody. Putting principle above people is to repeat the Pharisees' mistake.

My approach to adding a third worship service at St. Peter's was naive at best. I had failed to observe a fundamental management maxim — always bring your key supporters on board before embarking on anything new, especially if it might lead to controversy. I had not generated support for my idea among parish leaders in advance of my announcement — I had not even checked with most of them. Nor had I asked whether the increased attendance made the congregation feel uncomfortable. From the outset, parishioners were not enthusiastic about my idea:

"We've been waiting a long time for the church to be full and we like the crowded feeling."

"Does this mean grandparents and grandchildren will be worshiping at different times?"

"We don't want guitar music on Sundays."

"Nine o'clock is too early for me to get my children there."

Every time someone registered an objection, even if the intent was to be helpful, I defended my decision. I became inflexible and began to see people as either for me or against me. I didn't merely want to address a need in the parish. I wanted to get my way; I wanted to *win*. When winning becomes the main thing, losing is a sure thing. Even if I had held firm and insisted on retaining the service, I would have lost and the entire parish would have lost, because my intransigence would have undermined trust and goodwill. Some of that happened anyway.

Control is not an evil thing. Someone needs to make decisions, to give direction, and sometimes that person needs to be the pastor. The manner in which control is exercised, however, can be either good or bad, depending in large measure on motive. Jesus spoke of this in the Sermon on the Mount, where he dwelt more on inner motivations than on outward acts. People know when you are taking them seriously, honoring their feelings, and listening to them. Where this is the case, differences can often be transcended. Where it is not the case, people sense that they are being manipulated. They resist, and disputes arise over nothing.

I learned that getting my way is almost never the most important thing in the long run. We can and should act, based on the information available to us and always showing respect for others. But we are never in control. No matter how passionately I preach, how brilliantly I plan, how hard I work, how much I read or pray, I cannot dictate events or other people's behavior. Even when I do everything right, I cannot guarantee results.

The first step in Alcoholics Anonymous is also the first step to spiritual maturity: "We realized that we were powerless over alcohol and that our lives had become unmanageable." I eventually learned that it isn't just alcohol I'm powerless over — it's everything. But there is one who can manage my life. When I learned to submit my life to God, I was able to relax. Things may go well or poorly for me. My ideas may be accepted or rejected. I may or may not be offered the job I want. But God is in charge. The bumper sticker says, "God is my co-pilot." Well, actually God is the pilot and I am the co-pilot — most of the time, I hope. Sometimes I'm not even the co-pilot. Sometimes I'm not even a member of the crew. Sometimes I'm not even on the plane. But God is still in control. Problems occur only when I forget that.

 **Decisions**

Several years ago I was offered a job I had not sought. It was in a city I knew and loved. I would have received a hefty raise in pay, and the work would have been profoundly satisfying to me, including writing, editing, and dealing with some of the nation's most thoughtful and creative Christians. Pam and I would have moved closer to our aging mothers. After several weeks of agonizing prayer and discernment, I turned the position down. It was the most wrenching decision of my life. I was so close to accepting the position that I called the firm offering the job to accept it, but the person I needed to speak to was out. A few minutes later I had changed my mind.

My reasons for declining the position had to do with what I would have left behind. Not only were Pam and I happy in Alabama, but my leaving at that time would have been injurious to the parish. I had been there only four years, and we were in the midst of a major capital campaign to build a new church. The parish's recent growth had not yet jelled, and without consistent leadership, the building program could fizzle. I would have betrayed people who had embodied the love of God for me, people whom I had come to love. Had I left then, my conscience would have given me no peace. Today, a decade later, I have not once regretted my decision.

In reaching that decision, I learned some things about discerning the will of God.

Discernment is an ongoing process. When faced with a perplexing situation in the past, I had often prayed about it. Sometimes this was a sudden onslaught of prayer because my prayers prior to that time had been sporadic and perfunctory. It was like storming the gates to gain entrance when I had no prior relationship with the lord of the castle. Those on good terms with the lord of the castle have no need to storm the gates. Discernment works best when it is an intensification or focusing of an ongoing relationship. That is what I experienced in this decision. Routine praying, daily acts of surrender to the will of God, had readied my soul for discernment in this specific situation.

Devotional aids are helpful. Written prayers and other texts helped bring clarity and peace to my perplexed heart. When I awoke in the middle of the night, my stomach in knots about the decision looming before me, I found a number of texts that soothed me. Some were from the Prayer Book. Some were written by Francis of Assisi, Lancelot Andrewes, John Wesley, Thomas Merton, and other classic devotional authors. Three hymn texts in particular helped me: "Take my life, and let it be consecrated, Lord, to thee," "O Jesus, I have promised to serve thee to the end," and "Make me a captive, Lord, and then I shall be free." I read and prayed these and similar texts over and over again, and I believe this helped lead me to the right decision.

The will of God is a relationship, not a command. Although there is sometimes a right and a wrong decision, I suspect that it often doesn't matter what we decide because it is possible to live faithfully with either decision. In any case, the decision itself is never the most important thing. The presence of the risen Lord in our lives is more important than the solution to any problem, the answer to any question. It may, in fact, be the only answer we get. When we surrender our wills to God and allow Jesus to hold us in his arms, our dilemmas may remain unresolved, but their power to distress us is diminished. It is as if Jesus says to us, "Be still. I am with you and I am Lord. That is sufficient for you."

The normal Christian growth process, dying to self, cannot be bypassed. It's easy to ask God to show us what to do — but what if we are asked to sacrifice our heart's desire? Would we have prayed for guidance if we had known how much it would hurt?

God speaks through unexpected voices. When I have sought the will of God in a difficult matter, I have usually looked to the Bible (especially to the Psalms) and other devotional literature, and I have consulted persons whose spiritual credentials were of the highest pedigree. All that helps, but sometimes God speaks through an "ordinary" person, someone we don't think of as a spiritual expert at all — someone like my wife, Pam, for instance, who is one of the most spiritually sensitive people I know, but whose insight I often overlook or take for granted. After weeks of labored indecision, it was a casual remark from Pam that clarified for me the decision I needed to make. "Why don't you just call them and tell them no?" she asked. Pam was the voice of the Lord to me at that moment. On what other occasions, I wonder, could I have saved myself heartache and trouble if I'd heeded her wisdom?

The wrong decision may look extremely good. The devil dresses up in nice clothes and speaks with a smooth accent. The wrong road often appears the better, more desirable, more just, more noble route. Otherwise, it wouldn't be tempting. The devil tried that strategy three times when he tempted Jesus in the wilderness, and Jesus saw through it. He tries it on us as well, and we can see through it, too — but only if we have learned to look through the eyes of Jesus.

Doubt

As a youngster, I never doubted anything. In the 1950s, Shelbyville, Kentucky, was like many small Southern towns where everybody believed the same things. There was one Jewish family in our town, and I knew two or three Roman Catholics. They were said to believe some different, even spooky things, but I rarely ran into them. Even non-churchgoers, if they doubted the prevailing Protestant orthodoxy, kept their opinions to themselves. With everybody at least paying lip service to the same beliefs, it never occurred to me to question them.

Then I went to college and started doubting everything. Gambier, Ohio, was not Shelbyville, Kentucky. At Kenyon College, I met students and faculty who didn't believe any of the things I believed. Some even laughed at ideas I had taken for granted. I read books by existentialists, humanists, atheists, and people to whom God, if God existed, was of no concern. Although I now see this exposure to the world of ideas as a normal part of growing up, at the time it was painful for me. I felt as if the entire structure of my life was being dismantled brick by brick. My foundations were crumbling. I wanted to cling to the certainties of the past, but could not. A popular song from that era by Gene Raskin captured how I felt:

> Once upon a time there was a tavern
> Where we used to raise a glass or two.
> Remember how we laughed away the hours,
> And dreamed of all the great things we would do.

CHORUS:
Those were the days, my friend.
We thought they'd never end,
We'd sing and dance forever and a day;
We'd live the life we choose,
We'd fight and never lose,
For we were young and sure to have our way.

Then the busy years went rushing by us.
We lost our starry notions on the way.
If by chance I'd see you in the tavern,
We'd smile at one another and we'd say... (CHORUS)*

I yearned for the return of faith, and for some years thereafter I fought my doubts like a gladiator in the ring. When I began to think of ordination, I wondered whether a person who doubted some of the church's foundational teachings could in good conscience present himself for ordination. Wouldn't I be a fraud in the pulpit? I prayed even harder to God to remove my doubts, to give me the kind of rock-like faith I observed in some of my friends. But God did not do so. I was ordained, still wondering about everything, especially whether my doubts made me unfit for what I was undertaking.

As I approach old age, God has still not removed my doubts. Instead, he has taught me to live with them. I have learned to accept God as God comes to me, and that includes God's decision to grant me only a modest allotment of faith. At the same time I have learned to savor other spiritual gifts that God has granted me in abundance, things such as joy, hope, peace, and gratitude. I no longer question why God gives one person one thing and another person something else. My place is to accept what God gives me and to use those gifts to his glory.

I've also concluded that doubt is not really opposed to faith. The opposite of faith is indifference, and I've never been indifferent to God.

---

*Those Were the Days, words and music by Gene Raskin. TRO-© Copyright 1962 (Renewed) 1968 (Renewed) Essex Music, Inc., New York, NY. Used by permission.

Pam once told me, "Your doubts are all in your head, but in your gut you believe in God as deeply as anyone I know. You can't *not* believe in God. God is part of everything you think and do. You couldn't turn away from God if you wanted to." I hope that is true. I can't remember when I wasn't thinking of God — wondering about God, angry at God, tired of God, seeking God, questioning God, surrendering to God, laughing and playing with God.

For reasons I cannot know, God must want me to continue to muddle along with doubts in my head. Maybe they strengthen my character. When I have spoken of my doubts from the pulpit, parishioners have told me afterward that they appreciate hearing about them, because it seems to affirm them when they have doubts. I have come to see my doubts as spiritual mosquitoes, buzzing around my soul: I don't like them; I wish they'd go away; occasionally I can get rid of them for a short while by swatting at them. But most of the time, I put up with them and get on with my business in spite of them.

I no longer fight my doubts. That would give them an importance they do not deserve. Thomas à Kempis wrote, "Don't fight your own thoughts. Don't answer the doubts the devil has sent you. Trust God's words.... For the devil does not tempt and pester infidels and sinners. He is sure he owns them. It is the faithful and devout whom he tempts and worries in many ways."

So I let my doubts be and devote my time and energy to more positive things — loving and enjoying God and the world God has made. Sometimes I am also able to nudge someone else along the road to a place where he or she will turn and begin to love and enjoy God. If I can assist some lonely or despondent person to open his or her soul so that God can fill it with something of the joy, hope, peace, and gratitude God has given me, the doubts that continue to nag at me will have amounted to very little.

$\mathcal{E}$ _____ Energy

I've read several articles, some of them in secular publications, about clergy burnout. It happens. I know, because it happened to me. The surest sign of burnout is lack of energy. When I find myself going through the motions but not thinking about what I'm doing, staring at the page of a book without concentrating on the words, or sitting through a meeting or interview but not really listening to what other people say, I recognize it as an energy problem and an early tip-off to possible burnout.

In some respects clergy burnout is like burnout in other fields. Entering middle age, many men (and probably women too, though some of the dynamics would differ for women) feel trapped in unhappy situations. That exuberant "I can conquer the world" attitude of youth is long gone. They've climbed as high as they're going to climb in their profession, and they ask, with Peggy Lee, "Is that all there is?" When they begin to suspect the answer is yes, they grow tired, disillusioned, and cynical. Some men make a drastic (and often ill-considered) change at this point in their lives. Call it burnout; call it mid-life crisis. Whatever you call it, it's widespread and it's not limited to clergy.

Young people, in whatever profession, usually feel energetic, even omnipotent. I entered the ranks of the ordained in my mid-twenties, brimming with eager self-confidence. I set out to climb every mountain and ford every stream. Perhaps pastors ordained in midlife have already acquired a more accurate assessment of themselves, their clay feet having tripped them up in earlier careers, but most young people are still unfamiliar with their clay feet. I acknowledged in theory that I was both a finite being and a sinner, but those were mere intellectual concepts. In my gut, I felt unconquerable — and that was a set-up for disappointment.

In some respects, though, clergy burnout is unique. Pastors like to see themselves as shepherds and their parishes as sheep — that's what the word "pastor" (one who labors in a pasture) means — and the metaphor has some validity. But it is a limited validity, and at a deeper level, pastor and parishioners are all sheep. Clergy are told that Jesus saved the world, but deep inside we think we're supposed to save it, and that's where we get into trouble. My first glimmer of this came early in my career when I was mulling over a decision about whether to accept a new job offer. I prayed for guidance as I sat alone in the church, gazing at the stained glass window above the altar, which depicted the Good Shepherd holding a lamb in his arm. I had looked at that window hundreds of times and always felt humbled by it, since as a priest, I was the designated representative of Jesus with the particular flock known as St. John's Church. Then suddenly it was as if the window turned upside down, and I saw myself no longer as a stand-in for Jesus, but as the lamb carried in his arm. From that moment on, I began to identify less with the confident, commanding Jesus and more with the helpless, needy lamb. In later years, burnout and exhaustion occurred only when I forgot where I was in that picture.

Another part of the problem with clergy burnout is the unrealistic expectations many priests have about the church, expectations which the church itself often encourages. The church had been a place of spiritual growth and affirmation for us — otherwise we would not have sought ordination. The energy with which many of us begin our first job after seminary comes from the rosy-eyed expectations of our parish that we entertain. We tell ourselves it will be like an extended family — a healthy, functional, supportive extended family. People will love us and we will love them. Excitement about the church's mission can be assumed, and everyone will agree what that mission is. We soon learn, however, that the church is an institution which usually acts like any other institutions, be they government agencies, businesses, universities, or hospitals. Whatever it may say, an institution's first priority is self-preservation, and if necessary for their own survival, most institutions will run roughshod over people. The church often behaves that way, too, but it won't admit it. It thinks of itself as different from other institutions, uniquely beneficent. So there is often a great gulf between what the church says and what the church does. When clergy are caught in the middle and can't find a way out, they become angry. That can be part of clergy burnout.

I have more energy now, in my early retirement years, than I had at some points during my full-time working career. I believe that's because I have learned to accept the brokenness of the institutional church. Like every other institution, the church is run by human beings, which means it's run by sinners. The church falls short of the glory of God and needs redeeming just like everything else. This is the way human life is. All the time. Everywhere. Even in church. I realized I wouldn't change it, and I have also learned to accept the brokenness within myself. We clergy are numbered among the sinners who run the church. We too fall short of the glory of God. Sooner or later, we will blow it. Then we either grow cynical and burned out, or we fall to our knees.

Perhaps the problem among clergy is that we usually don't know how to fall to our knees. Many seminaries do not teach this. The church has focused its energy on liturgical reform, social problems, and institutional maintenance. These are important, but we will avoid the disillusionment, cynicism, and exhaustion of burnout only when we learn to surrender our wills to God. I learned it the hard way. Maybe that's the only way.

Father

As an adult, I always lived far away from my parents, so I saw my
father just two or three times a year. Those visits became increasingly
tense for me, largely because of alcohol. Like me, my father was an
alcoholic, but unlike me, he never entered recovery. When we were
both drinking, we argued about politics and religion, neither of us
listening to the other, each biding his time as the other spoke, thinking
of the next clever one-liner with which to shoot down the other's
position. I thought my father didn't love me, and I thought I didn't
love him. I remember imagining a brick wall behind which I placed
my father so that his remarks and behaviors would not hurt me. But
they did hurt, and I grew angry, although I didn't know I was angry
because I didn't *feel* angry. For years I kept my anger at my father
behind that brick wall. My entry into alcoholism recovery, three years
before my father's death, added a sense of guilt for not having staged
an intervention to bring my father into recovery. An intervention
initiated by me wouldn't have worked, but I felt guilty just the same.

Then my father died. I learned of his death at 10:55 p.m. on Christmas Eve, 1985. My brother telephoned me at St. Peter's, Ladue, where
I was standing in the undercroft, vested and ready to process into the
church five minutes later to preach and celebrate the Christmas Eve
Eucharist. He told me Dad had died earlier that evening, of a massive
coronary. I immediately envisioned a telephone set on which I men-
tally pressed the hold button — I would deal with this later. I didn't
react to Dad's death that evening, and people in the parish told me

afterward that they admired the calm way I conducted the Christmas Eve service, having just received such news. They didn't know about that imaginary wall behind which I had confined my feelings for my father, out of sight and out of mind where they couldn't get at me. Not crying was easy for me that Christmas Eve. I left my feelings for my father on hold, behind that wall, for nearly a year thereafter, shedding not one tear for him during that time.

For years I had had trouble reading the parable of the Prodigal Son without crying. The tears always came at this point: "But while the son was yet at a distance, his father saw him and had compassion, and ran and embraced him and kissed him." I had not forgotten the time, years earlier, when my father had seen me from a distance and had run to embrace and kiss me. It was the year following my graduation from college. Confused, without direction, and without a job, I was living alone in a small, windowless basement flat in Columbus, Ohio, a city where I knew no one. I wanted to go home, but that would not have solved my problems. One evening when I was at my lowest point, I telephoned my parents just to hear the voice of someone who loved me. I do not now recall what I told them, but five hours later, my father was on my doorstep, having driven the two hundred miles to Columbus from our home in Kentucky and canceling everything on his schedule for that evening and the next day. But as alcohol began to affect how we related to one another, such expressions of caring ceased between us.

Several things have become clear to me as I have reflected on my relationship to my father. The first is that my feelings about God are tied to my feelings about my father. I read once that a person's relationship to God is often conditioned by his relationship to his father. Those who experience their fathers as warm and loving will think of God the same way; those who experience their fathers as cold and distant will think of God the same way. A father who is absent or present, reliable or unreliable, predictable or unpredictable, generous or stingy, winsome or stern, will condition his children to look for the same thing in God. I always knew my father would be loyal to me — loyalty was his defining virtue — but I grew more and more severed from him emotionally. During the last fifteen years of his life, I was sure the love we had once felt for each other had dried up completely. At that time I also came to think of God as emotionally distant from me.

Another thing I have learned from my relationship to my father is that my personal life cannot be separated from my professional life. The months following my father's death were full of unfocused tension, confusion, anger, and loneliness. This was partly because of my inability to come to terms with his death. My relationship to my parish became strained as St. Peter's became for me a kind of father substitute. Psychologists call this "transference." When I was unable to acknowledge my feelings about my father, I projected them onto my parish. I thought my parish did not love me. I became angry over real and imagined slights. I withdrew emotionally. Upon leaving St. Peter's in March 1988, I even wrote a piece for a theological journal addressing my parish as a parent. In later years, when I felt myself becoming angry at someone in my parish, I learned to look for something closer to home that was bothering me and which I was reluctant to examine, resulting in my projecting my feelings onto someone else.

Similarly, I saw how parishioners who are tense or angry over something unrelated to the church — marital, family, financial, or job-related problems — can project their feelings onto the church, often onto the pastor personally. It may feel too dangerous to confront one's spouse or boss, but the pastor (or the bishop or the national church office) is a safe target. On occasion I found myself serving as a kind of lightning rod, attracting parishioners' free-floating anger, often in the form of unfounded accusations or exaggerated reactions to things I did or said. When I was aware of this dynamic, it became easier for me to accept the anger and not to become angry in return.

In the same article in which I addressed my parish as a parent, I also addressed it as a child. Just as I sometimes felt like the child, with the parish as nurturing and disciplining parent, at other times I felt like the parent, with the parish as willful, infuriating, winsome, immature, adorable child. When I got into trouble in parish ministry, it was often because I tried to play the part of the child when the parish needed to be guided and disciplined, or I tried to play the part of the parent when I was the one needing guidance and discipline.

In November 1986, eleven months after my father's death, I took part in a workshop on alcoholism intervention at the diocesan conference center. Part of the event was a role-playing exercise. I volunteered to play the alcoholic. Others in the group took the roles of my wife, children, and colleagues. They spoke of their love for me and their concern about my drinking. Then the tears came. I sobbed uncontrollably for twenty minutes. The workshop leader stopped the exercise, fearing that I was experiencing a nervous breakdown. Through my sobbing, I said, "I'm all right. My tears are real and I'm not acting, but it's all right. I'm crying for my father, that he never sat in this chair and never heard these things from those who loved him. And I'm crying out of gratitude that my own wife and children will never need to say these things to me." It was then I realized I loved my father.

Some time after my father's death, I was praying alone in the church one morning. I had often addressed God in my prayers as "heavenly Father." That morning a voice in the back of my head seemed to say, "Why do you always call me 'Father'? Why don't you call me 'Daddy'?"

I remembered that the Aramaic *abba*, the word Jesus used when addressing God, was an intimate name rather than a formal word, more like "daddy" than "father." I tried praying to my "heavenly Daddy." It felt awkward and presumptuous, but I am slowly learning to address God more intimately. I am also learning to envision myself sitting in my earthly father's lap, held in his strong and loving arms, something I experienced as a young child but later forgot. I now believe both my father and I would have enjoyed such intimacy throughout our lives if either of us had known how to ask the other for it.

Reflecting on my relationship to my father has also helped me become a better father. One of the greatest gifts my father gave me was the freedom to be myself. He saw that I had an excellent education but intentionally steered me toward a college other than the one from which he had graduated, although he had loved his school. He never pressured me to enter the family soft-drink bottling business — I would have been the fourth generation of Schmidt men to do so — or to settle in Kentucky to care for him and my mother in their old age. My father wanted me to become the person God intended me to be, not a reflection of himself. This cannot have been easy for him, especially when my political views took a leftish turn, but he held fast to his conviction that I should be my own man, and I am grateful to him for it. It has also not been easy for me to let my own sons be themselves, especially when they make decisions I would not have made, but I remember my father's great gift of freedom to me, and I hope I am doing as well by my sons as my father did by me.

I am like my father in more ways than our shared alcoholism. Most of what I received from my father has been a great blessing to me — a sense of loyalty to and responsibility for my wife and children, a concern for the well-being of the larger community, a commitment to what is right, a love of music and of baseball, a willingness to work hard, and most of all, my faith in God. I have my father to thank for all that. I see now that my father was a very good man, a noble man, who suffered toward the end of his life from a disease that killed him. Today, after the passage of nearly two decades, I know that my father loved me and that I loved him. I love him still, and I am proud that as I grow older, I bear an increasingly marked physical resemblance to him.

Forgiveness

People who say to "forgive and forget" are suggesting the impossible. You can't forgive *and* forget; it's one or the other. If I forget a wound or a slight, it was negligible or unimportant to me. Such hurts don't require forgiveness because they are quickly put behind. Forgetting is easy. Forgiveness is something else, and it is hard. A struggle precedes forgiveness, and forgiveness is necessary or possible only where a profound betrayal has occurred. Even when I have managed to reach the point of forgiveness, I have never forgotten and I never could forget. Deep wounds, even when forgiven, are remembered.

When I shared the story of my recovery from alcoholism in confidence with a woman in my parish, she betrayed my confidence, thereby damaging my reputation in the community. It took me several years to forgive her. Uncharitable thoughts of the woman often invaded my mind, and I rehearsed caustic speeches to her while driving alone in my car. That felt good to me, but what was even more satisfying was imagining myself overhearing the speeches of others as they defended my honor to her. I found expressions of revenge in the Bible that were hardly sweet, but which I chewed upon with pleasure. The anonymous authors of Psalms 69 and 109 knew how I felt and said it so well.

> Let their eyes be darkened, that they may not see,
> and give them continual trembling in their loins. (69:25)

Or:

> Let there be no one to show him kindness,
> and none to pity his fatherless children. (109:11)

But then I realized that although those psalmists had expressed my thoughts, they weren't people I'd have wanted to associate with. I pictured them marinating in self-pity. Could that be me? Did people not want to associate with me either? Could my most dangerous enemy be not the woman spreading rumors about me, but the enemy within, the foul spirit poisoning my soul?

Jesus said to forgive our enemies. Did Jesus go through such mental wrestling? Did he debate in his heart whether to forgive or curse his enemies, as I had done? Did Jesus have an enemy within? Loving someone who has wronged us is difficult, to be sure, but loving the enemy within us is even more difficult. Did Jesus understand this? I began to realize it is precisely the enemy within whom Christ loves, forgives, and transforms, probably including the enemy within his own heart. An old hymn by Charlotte Elliott came to mind. Miss Elliott was an invalid who felt worthless because of her inability to do anything for God. Then the words of her famous hymn came to her:

> Just as I am, though tossed about
> with many a conflict, many a doubt;
> fightings and fears within, without,
>   O Lamb of God, I come, I come. . . .
> Just as I am: thou wilt receive;
>   wilt welcome, pardon, cleanse, relieve,
> because thy promise I believe,
>   O Lamb of God, I come, I come.

I sang that hymn over and over to myself, asking that Christ "welcome, pardon, cleanse, relieve" my resentment. Gradually I came to know that I, a sinner burdened by self-pity and self-righteousness, was welcomed into the arms of Christ. Accepted by Christ, I was then able to accept myself as well. I came to love my enemy within. That enemy even became a friend of sorts, for an enemy recognized and pardoned becomes an ally who helps us understand the enemy in others.

But what of the woman? Jesus had said to pray for our enemies, so I prayed for her. Grudgingly. Gritting my teeth. The words stuck in my throat. Perhaps those prayers helped her, but they didn't seem to be helping me, at least not that I could discern. Despite my praying, my resentment of her persisted. But very gradually, as I began to understand Christ's acceptance of me, I began also to understand his acceptance of her, and I came to see her as a child of God with spiritual troubles of her own. My resentment finally vanished, like the water on a concrete floor that has been hosed down. You sweep the water away, but it returns time and again to the low spot on the floor, until finally, when you've swept it away for the hundredth time, it has evaporated and is gone for good. I prayed my resentment away again and again, and it stayed away for just a moment, until finally, one day, I prayed it away and it did not return. I had come to see that I could not condemn the woman when Christ had so freely embraced us both. I ceased fantasizing about getting even with her and began to accept her and her behavior. I even began to want good things for her — healing, self-acceptance, joy.

Thomas Merton said that it is not enough to forgive others; we must forgive them with humility and compassion. I take that to mean that we are to acknowledge that some and perhaps most of the fault is our own. To forgive with humility means to admit we may have nothing to forgive. After all the cursing, all the blaming, all the self-righteous indignation, it may turn out that forgiveness is something we must ask from others rather than offer to others. Perhaps others have wronged us and perhaps not, but if we focus on other people's misdoings, we block out humility and compassion. We must let go of all that. Only then will we have forgiven as Christ has forgiven us.

One of my most humbling yet happiest memories is of a Sunday morning in my Alabama parish when the church was overflowing. In the back of the room was one of my closest friends, a grandmother from the parish, accompanied by her son and his family — including noisy grandchildren — visiting from out of town. The noise grated on my nerves. At the peace, I walked to the rear of the church and asked the family if they would like me to request an usher to take their youngsters to the nursery. It was one of the rudest things I've ever done. The grandmother and parents were mortified and quickly left the church. I realized immediately that I had overstepped the bounds of kindness and decency. I apologized after church and wrote notes of apology the next day. To my surprise and great relief, the grandmother accepted my apology. She did not excuse my behavior, and I'm sure she will never forget it, but neither did she allow my rudeness to become the defining thing in our relationship. She was, for that particular week, Christ to me — welcoming, pardoning, cleansing, relieving — and our friendship continues to this day.

As the priest who pronounces absolution, the declaration of God's forgiveness, following the congregation's confession of sin, I try always to remember that I am only secondarily God's spokesman and representative. First of all, I am a member of the congregation, and when I pronounce the absolution, I speak to myself.

Fun

Why do so many Christians prefer heaviness to lightness, severity to gentleness, gloom to joy? Why do we transform the Christian gospel from an invitation to enjoy God into an injunction to endure God? When God says, "Come and dance with me," why do we hear, "Depart and work for me"?

One of the churches I served had a large bell in the steeple above the balcony. The bell's rope hung down through a hole in the ceiling. Every Sunday before the main service, I walked up the stairs into the balcony and rang the bell. I pulled as hard as I could, several times, until the bell turned far enough on its axle to ring. When the bell fell back, it pulled the rope up into the air, and if you held the rope tightly, it would lift you off your feet. One Sunday morning, I saw a mother and her seven-year-old son, David, sitting in the balcony. David eyed me as I pulled on the rope. I beckoned to him, and he leaped to me over the back of the pew. "Would you like to ring the bell?" I said. David glowed with anticipation. "You may ring it, and if you hold on tightly, the rope will carry you up into the air. You must not let go, or you will fall to the floor, but I'll stand here to catch you in case you do let go. Now pull hard, David, and hold on!" He did, and he rose into the air, happy as a lark. I saw his mother out of the corner of my eye. She was frowning. Then she said, in a loud whisper which I'm sure I was meant to overhear, "David, we are *in church!*" I felt scolded. Was having fun in church against the rules?

It was then that I began to question some things many churches take for granted. Church music, I decided, doesn't have to be serious music. The architecture doesn't have to consist of pointed arches and ornate moldings. Sermons can include personal humor. Children are to be welcome everywhere, all the time — well, mostly everywhere, most of the time, anyway. Announcements can be an occasion for light-hearted banter. Liturgical vestments and ceremonial, which would seem peculiar or silly anywhere else, are peculiar and silly in church as well, and it's all right to laugh at them. Jesus, I decided, could be funny. We don't think of Jesus as funny because we've been taught to see him as grave, mild, and endlessly patient. But Jesus often used irony and hyperbole in his teaching, and many of his stories and sayings surely brought smiles to the faces of his listeners. And then there is what we actually do in church: what could be crazier than receiving God in the form of stamped-out unleavened bread and a sip of port? In fact, the whole church business is crazy, unlikely, bizarre, and funny. So why not enjoy it?

A woman came into my office one day to discuss her faith. She had worshiped in several churches in the area, but without believing much of what she'd heard there. The doubting had bothered her, and she had worked hard to find the truth and monitor her progress. At my parish, she told me, she had found a community where she felt free to be herself, including her doubts, without being judged. Yet she still felt a heaviness within her, something she called "shame."

"It sounds as if you don't know how to enjoy God," I said. She said she had never thought of that. The God she'd known could be worshiped, served, obeyed — but *enjoyed?*

As a child, I learned part of the Westminster Catechism. The first question was, "What is the chief end of man?" The answer: "The chief end of man is to glorify God and enjoy him forever." I've never forgotten those words, but at times, like the woman who came to my office that day, I've thought of God as a stern judge and of myself as God's bondsman. When such thoughts have lodged in my soul, it has been difficult either to glorify or to enjoy God.

Two days after talking with the woman, I celebrated the Ash Wednesday liturgy. That's a service fraught with penitence, and I noticed for the first time how joyful Ash Wednesday penitence is meant to be. The service incorporates two psalms. Psalm 51 is known for its searing consciousness of sin and its pleading to be washed, purged, blotted clean. It is easy to overlook the fact that what the psalmist asks for is the return of joy, something he apparently once knew but had forgotten. "Make me hear of joy and gladness.... Give me the joy of your saving help again," he prays. The other Ash Wednesday psalm is Psalm 103, which, despite repeated references to the psalmist's sins, infirmities, wickedness, and mortality, rings with joy. It refers repeatedly to God's loving mercy and reiterates the line, "Bless the Lord, O my soul." That is because in the midst of pain, suffering, and contrition, the psalmist experiences God as good. Even the Proper Preface for Lent refers to the season as a time of *joyful* preparation.

The key to enjoying God is humility, but not the kind of humility that cowers and grovels, loudly proclaiming its awfulness. Focusing entirely on self, that sort of humility is actually a form of spiritual pride. Real humility is acceptance of self, including both abilities and shortcomings, good and bad, body and spirit, the noble and the ridiculous. It conducts a spiritual inventory from time to time, but without spending long hours studying its face in the mirror. It focuses on God, not self, and eventually becomes confident and relaxed in God's grace, enjoying God, even playing with God, even laughing and joking with God. There should be more of that in church.

_G_ _____ Guilt

"That sermon made me feel guilty." I didn't often hear that remark when people spoke to me as they left church, but I remember one Sunday when I heard it several times. The topic of my sermon that day was, not surprisingly, tithing. "My family and I tithe, and I think you should, too," I had said, with more directness than was my usual custom. Several things had caused me to speak so bluntly. For one thing, I had read a news article that said the typical middle-class American was part of the wealthiest 2 percent of the planet's population. I was also tired of people whose gift to the church came out of what was left after they bought their big houses and luxury automobiles saying, "We give all we can." Then there were the remarks of Jesus: "Where your treasure is, there will your heart be also. . . . Lay not up for yourselves treasures on earth. . . . Woe to you that are rich" — not much room for mistaking the thrust of that. And besides, it was October, time for the annual Every Member Canvass. Was I trying to use guilt to squeeze money out of people? I would have denied it. My motive in speaking that way was, I would have said, to encourage people to adopt a practice that had brought joy and contentment into my own life. But perhaps I was feeling angry because people weren't doing what I wanted, and maybe I did want to make them feel guilty.

Guilt is a slippery word. It is often used to refer to a feeling. When people say, "I want to get rid of my guilt," they may mean they want to rid themselves of negative feelings. But how people feel about themselves has as much to do with psychology — or with what they ate for lunch — as with their relationship to God. A clever speaker can sometimes induce a guilty feeling in others (preachers and mothers are good at this), but the feeling may have nothing to do with objective reality, with actual sin. Everybody is a sinner — "All have sinned and fallen short of the glory of God," as St. Paul said — so real guilt (as distinguished from the feeling of guilt) is universal. We're all guilty, no matter how we feel about ourselves.

There are various ways to stop feeling guilty. Therapy, exercise, and dropping out of church have been known to work. But there is only one way to get rid of actual guilt, and that is to receive the loving God deep in our hearts, to accept God's forgiveness and grace, and to let God remake us into new persons. This is astonishingly hard for most people to do, because we seem to have been programmed to think of God as exacting Judge rather than as transforming Redeemer. How this programming came to infect the Christian church, I don't know. I'm sure it was the work of the devil, but how the devil did it is beyond me. God is our Judge, of course, but if that's all we know of God, we have entirely missed the point of Jesus Christ.

A woman came to see me once, walking hesitantly, hunched over, ashen in the face. At first I thought she had suffered some calamity. But as she began to talk, I realized that the outward circumstances of her life were pleasant enough — her pain came from within. "I just can't believe that God could actually forgive me," she said. I asked whether she had done something terrible. "Nothing," she said. "I just feel so rotten and dirty and unworthy inside. God couldn't possibly love me." As we talked, she told me the story of her life, including a severe religious upbringing full of censure, condemnation, and sexual abuse by churchgoing relatives.

I opened the Prayer Book to the Collect for Ash Wednesday and read it to her. "That says God hates nothing that he has made, which

includes you. Do you believe that?" I asked. She mumbled that she
did not believe it. I realized the woman had two related but different
problems. One was her feeling of guilt. After seeing her two more
times, I referred her to a therapist in the parish to deal with her
negative feelings about herself. Her other problem was actual guilt.
Like all people, she was guilty, but God does not want us to carry the
burden of our guilt — and the woman had no inkling of that. I saw
her a few more times to help her open herself up to the love of God.

In our final session, I asked her to visualize the scene in heaven
when she stands before the Lord. "And what do you think Jesus will say
to you when you see him face to face?" I asked her. She sat stone-faced
and did not respond.

I then asked her to think of Jesus speaking to her in this vein:

> I've made a note of every time you cussed. Every time you made a
> catty remark, I wrote it down. Whenever you kicked the dog, smoked
> a cigarette, passed by a beggar, yelled at your children, missed church,
> fudged on your taxes, nagged your husband, read a bawdy book, forgot
> to write a thank-you note, I put it down next to your name. It's all
> written down right here in this ledger book. I've got enough on you to
> send you up the river for good. I've had to add so many pages to your
> ledger book that I can hardly lift it up here on the table to add up the
> columns!
>
> But no matter. I only kept your ledger book so that I could have the
> fun of watching your face as I tore it up. *Rip!* There goes that page.
> *Slash! Tear!* There go two more. Lots of you work yourselves up into
> a real sickness trying to make a passing score on this, and you feel all
> guilty and heavy when you realize you've failed. Or you feel smug when
> you think you've passed. Then you arrive up here and see me ripping
> up the books and throwing the pages away. It's such fun to watch your
> reactions.
>
> Some people object and claim the whole business isn't fair. You've
> worked hard to be good, you tell me, and you want credit. When I hear
> that, it makes me sad. But some of you just start laughing and giggling
> when you realize the important thing isn't what you've done or not
> done, but who I am and who you are. I am Love and you are Beloved.

I kept your ledger book all these years just so that I could tear it up when we finally met face to face. Welcome home, my Beloved!

My conversations with the woman occurred in a different parish and several years after I had preached the sermon on tithing that made people feel guilty. I like to think I had learned some things in the intervening years and that I would not have spoken as I did in the sermon had I preached it some years later. The points about Christian stewardship in the sermon were and remain valid, I believe, but there are better ways to address those issues. If the sermon's goal was to use guilt to motivate increased giving to the church, it didn't work, because the canvass that fall resulted in only a slight increase in pledges over the year before, but even if people had doubled their giving because they felt guilty, their relationship to God would not have become more free and joyful because of it. Most people are either burdened by imaginary guilt or oblivious to their genuine guilt, and self-righteous posturing from the pulpit doesn't help any of them. What helps is to identify the love of God manifest in people's lives and to conduct our personal and professional affairs accordingly. That opens up possibilities for God to transform people, and when God does that, people give generously no matter what preachers say.

 **Homeless**

Most of my ministry was in suburban parishes. That meant if I encountered a homeless person, I usually had to make a point of doing so.

Four years at St. John's Episcopal Church in downtown Charleston, West Virginia, was my only experience of urban ministry. During my last year at St. John's, the parish opened a soup kitchen that fed homeless people at the church every day of the year, but before that, the homeless often stopped by St. John's asking for a handout — for food, a night's lodging, a bus ticket. Each person's story began the same way: "Father, I'm an Episcopal and I don't like asking for money, but...." No Episcopalian would call himself an "Episcopal," so I knew that part of the story was concocted and suspected the rest was, too. But surely not everyone was lying, and how was I to know who was telling the truth? Believing it better to help someone who didn't need it than to refuse help to someone who did, I tried to help everyone (but never with cash). Invariably, the recipient of my handout would promise to pay me back as soon as he was able, and with that in mind, I gave each person a card with the mailing address of the church. But I never expected anything to come from it.

I was surprised in this only once. A particularly dirty and smelly transient stopped by the church and told what I thought was a preposterous tale: "Father, I'm an Episcopal and I don't like asking for money, but I've written a television commercial that I'm trying to sell to a station, and as soon as I sell it, I'll be on my feet again. I've been on the road from Chicago, to Indianapolis, to Louisville, to Lexington, to Huntington, and now to Charleston, but I haven't sold my commercial. Roanoke is the next town with a TV station. Can I borrow the money for a bus ticket to Roanoke so I can try to sell my commercial there? I'll pay you back when I sell my commercial." *An unusually creative tale*, I thought. I knew that his geography was right, but I didn't believe a word he said. I bought him a nonrefundable one-way bus ticket to Roanoke and gave him one of the church's cards, sure I'd never hear from him again. Ten days later, I was astonished to receive in the mail a hand-addressed envelope, with a Roanoke postmark, containing a postal money order for twice what I had spent for the man's bus ticket and a note that read, "Father, I sold my commercial in Roanoke. Here's the money you lent me, plus enough for you to help the next person. Thank you and God bless you."

A few years later I was rector of Christ Church in Fairmont, West Virginia. The parish decided to feed Thanksgiving dinner to the town's homeless population. Dozens of parishioners donated food and money, publicized the event in local news media, arranged for transportation to the church for those without cars, set places for a hundred guests at dinner tables in the parish hall, and prepared a full Thanksgiving dinner in the church's kitchen. Everything was ready at noon on Thanksgiving Day, with eighteen parishioners ready to serve the meal and a clean-up crew due to arrive at 1:00.

The only thing lacking, it turned out, was the guests. Actually, guests were not entirely lacking — seven showed up. They had second and third helpings of turkey and dressing, cranberries, potatoes, garden peas, rolls and butter, pumpkin and mincemeat pies. They took more food home for supper that night, and they seemed appreciative. Two of the seven were clients at the school for retarded adults that met regularly at Christ Church during the week. Another was an elderly woman with no family who arrived an hour early and stayed until the last dish was put away.

"After the shock wore off and we nursed our deflated egos, I think we were glad we'd done what we did," said Kevin Rengers, the parishioner who had coordinated the project. "We learned that some people are embarrassed at having to walk into the church for a free meal. They aren't comfortable here. I think a better way would be to prepare dinner at the church and deliver hot dinners to people. That would also mean we'd have to figure out where to find them, and then maybe we'd learn some other things about them, and maybe Thanksgiving Day turkey would be just the beginning." A couple of years later, Christ Church parishioners led an ecumenical effort to open a local food pantry, which now serves hundreds of people every month of the year.

Ladue, Missouri, feels far removed from the homeless people of nearby St. Louis, but parishioners of St. Peter's Episcopal Church in Ladue have developed a singular ministry to the homeless. As rector of St. Peter's, I convened a group of parishioners and asked them to devise a project that met three criteria: It should (1) address a genuine need in the St. Louis area, (2) engage St. Peter's parishioners personally as well as financially, and (3) produce visible results before initial enthusiasm could fade away. Beyond that, I gave the group no suggestions.

The results of that little initiative astonished me. Within a year, the group had bought a rubble-filled shell of a building on St. Louis's north side, converted it into a bright and comfortable residence hall, and created the Haven of Grace, a shelter for pregnant homeless women from the streets of the city. St. Peter's parishioners initially contributed money, supplies, and two thousand hours of labor, and many parishioners volunteered at the Haven of Grace during the years that followed, cleaning, moving furniture, counseling, keeping the books, providing legal advice, running the food bank, doing carpentry, hanging wallpaper, taking pictures, providing pre- and post-natal medical care, leading job-training seminars, delivering supplies, raising funds, and handling public relations. Best of all was that apart from putting together the initial committee, I had almost nothing to do with it. The people of St. Peter's created the Haven of Grace and operate it to this day.

Several years later, Linda Mayson, a parishioner of mine at St. Paul's, Daphne, phoned to ask whether I'd like to help the United Way of Mobile count the city's homeless people. Accurate data would help in providing services to the homeless. I was one of about fifty volunteers who divided into teams of five persons, and we set out at eight in the evening. My team consisted of two veteran street people (an out-of-work electrician and a former — at least that's what she said — hooker), a Roman Catholic nun, a college intern, and myself. The neighborhood assigned to us consisted of most of downtown Mobile. We wore identifying badges, carried flashlights, and phoned the United Way office every hour to report on our location and that we were safe. By the time the night ended, my feet felt as if I'd walked from Mobile to Baton Rouge. We had found fifty homeless persons, walking aimlessly along the street, sitting in fast food restaurants, holed up in abandoned buildings, and sleeping under bridges, behind shrubbery, and on porches and rooftops.

I discovered several things that night. I learned that homeless people constitute a community. The two street people on our team recognized nearly all the homeless people we came across. They not only knew their names, but where to find them and which ones we'd find in which places. Homeless people care for one another, protect one another, and survive by sharing what they have. I also learned that life on the street can be brutal. Many homeless people, male and female, resort to prostitution to earn a few dollars, and they are continually threatened by thugs who attack them and steal their meager belongings. But the homeless themselves, I discovered, pose no threat, and most of them are not angry at the world. I was also struck by the intelligence of many homeless people, not merely streetwise intelligence, but scholastic learning as well. A number of the people I met were witty, articulate, and urbane. One man who lived beneath a viaduct of Interstate 10 was sitting under a streetlight reading E. M. Forster's *A Passage to India* when we approached him. And I learned that like other people, homeless people appreciate genuine kindness — a police officer who knows where they sleep and stops while making his rounds to inquire who might need something; a night watchman who, against his company's rules, invites a couple of people to sleep in his heated office on cold nights; a restaurant manager who gives out freshly cooked meals before closing up at two in the morning.

Lots of thoughts about homeless people hang in my mind, most without answers: Who were these people's parents? Do they have wives or husbands? Are they parents, and if so, where are their children? Do expressions like "the love of Christ" and "the grace of God," which flow so easily off my lips, have any meaning for them? As a man with a relatively large income, what is my responsibility to them? Have I done my part by walking through the streets of Mobile one night every year? Does sending a regular check off to the local food pantry discharge my responsibility? Does society at large have a responsibility to its individual members? What does God think of homeless people? What does God think of those with comfortable homes who blame homeless people for being on the streets? What should my parish's priorities be in formulating our operating budget and allocating our resources of time and talent? If Jesus were here now, where would he spend the night?

One final thought: The Bible contains a good story about ministry to homeless people. Although he is often overlooked (I've never seen a crèche scene that includes him), maybe the real hero of the Christmas story is the innkeeper.

Homosexuality

Two hot controversies had dragged on for a decade and exhausted the Episcopal Church by 1976. One concerned the adoption of a revised Prayer Book and the other concerned ordaining women to the priesthood. Both were resolved that year. It was also in 1976 that a friend said to me, "You know what the next hot issue will be, don't you?" No, I didn't. In fact, I'd hoped for a respite from hot issues. "It will be gays, the ordination of gays," he said, "and it will make what we've gone through with the Prayer Book and women priests seem like a Mitch Miller sing-along." I couldn't imagine ordaining a gay person, but I agreed that if such an ordination were ever proposed, the controversy would be hotter than anything we'd seen before.

And so it has been, for the last quarter of a century. The battle began soon after my friend made his comment to me. Three years later, I found myself signing a petition, along with twenty-five other priests from the Diocese of West Virginia, stating that ordaining sexually active gay people was contrary to church discipline. Eleven other priests and two laypersons signed a different petition affirming the opposing view.

As I look over those two lists of names today, I recall my close friendships with those who had signed both petitions. It was a time when friends could differ on this question and remain friends. That became more difficult in the two decades that followed. A hint of what was to come could be seen in a letter to the editor of the diocesan newspaper in which the two petitions appeared. It referred to two "parties or philosophies" in the church, one of which the author called "dilutionists," who wanted to "water down the gospel to make it acceptable to all people at all costs," and the other of which he called "catholic traditionalists," who adhered to Christian teaching "as the Bible and the church have always understood it." The era of name-calling had begun. Both sides proved gifted at it. On the one side were the "revisionist, heretical, radical, relativist, biblically illiterate secular humanists." On the other were the "ignorant, simplistic, fundamentalist, homophobic, rigid biblical literalists." Each of these terms was slung like a stone, intended to hit and wound those on the other side. It seemed everyone wanted to shout and no one wanted to listen. The place of gays in the church came up repeatedly at regional and national church gatherings, and even during lulls in the name-calling, the air was tense. Church meetings ceased to be enjoyable reunions where everyone was an old friend; friends were now limited to those with whom you agreed on the gay issue.

I remember one especially painful moment. It was in the summer of 1991, when, at my suggestion, the vestry of St. Paul's Church, Daphne, passed a resolution to be forwarded to our diocese's deputies to the Episcopal Church's General Convention, then in session in Phoenix. It acknowledged that the church was divided over the questions of gay ordination and same-sex unions and asked the deputies from the Central Gulf Coast to vote for measures that would respect persons of different views, on both the left and the right, and avoid legislation that would make anyone feel marginalized or excluded. This would allow the whole church time — it might take many years, we thought — to pray and learn until the truth became clear to all and consensus was reached. In a word, we were asking the church to *wait*. The St. Paul's vestry received an unexpected response from the senior warden of a nearby Episcopal parish. He wrote a three-page, single-spaced letter excoriating us in demeaning, sarcastic terms that took name-calling to a new low. Although he demanded a response, the St. Paul's vestry wisely declined to respond, because the letter had not been an invitation to conversation but a childish tirade leaving no room for conversation. One vestry member did respond privately, questioning how a Christian could use such language, especially when addressing other Christians.

My views about gays changed over the years. By 1991, I would no longer have signed the petition I had signed in West Virginia in 1979. What changed my mind? Two things, one intellectual and the other personal. The intellectual change came from my studying the scripture passages referring to homosexuality and my reading of scientific literature. It appears to me that the Bible gives no clear guidance on same-sex unions. The few references to homosexuality in the Bible are all negative, but of questionable applicability. The clearest condemnations of homosexuality are found in Leviticus 18:22 and 20:13, part of the Holiness Code, a long document that the Christian church has usually regarded as applicable only to ancient Judaism. The Genesis creation story refers to humankind being created "male and female," but it is unlikely the author of that story was trying to make a statement about sexual orientation when he wrote those words. Other often-cited passages seem to have been written about temple prostitution, pederasty, hedonistic passion, or some other behavior that little resembles a mature, committed union of any kind. The other two traditional sources of authority for Anglicans, tradition and reason, are also inconclusive, I find (though most of the church's tradition weighs in on the negative side). Add to this the scientific studies that seem to suggest (the evidence is not all in) that sexual orientation may be at least partly genetic — like height, hair color, and left- or right-handedness — and I cannot rule out the blessing of same-sex unions and the ordination of qualified gay and lesbian persons. For a time I didn't know what to make of the testimonies of those claiming to have been "cured" of homosexuality through prayer. I have no reason to doubt these testimonies. It is likely, I think, that those who are changed from gay to straight through prayer are persons whose sexual orientation is borderline rather than profound. Others have prayed fervently to be made heterosexual and their prayers have not been granted.

On a more personal level, I came to know several gay persons well, and their witness had an impact on me. In Philadelphia, my wife, sons, and I were very fond of a particular priest. One day the priest and I had occasion to ride in a car together for two hours. During our ride, he confided to me that he was gay. "I have never told any member of my parish," he said, "because I know they wouldn't understand. In fact, you are the first straight person I have ever told. The burden of living a double life has been almost too much for me to bear. I can't tell you what relief I feel just to tell *one* straight person and know that you will still be my friend." Tears were running down his cheek. He then told of years of healing services, prayer ministries, charismatic praise meetings, psychotherapy, and repeated private pleas to God to change his sexual orientation. Finally, he said, at the age of fifty, he had accepted that he was gay. He said he had a male friend on the other side of the city whom he saw once or twice a month. Long before I had learned my friend was gay, I had known him to be a conscientious, prayerful, effective parish priest. Knowing him as I did, I could not believe that God was not glorified when my friend served at the altar.

Most of my other gay friends have been members of the parishes I served. All were discreet about their sexual orientation, especially where the community might not have welcomed their going public. Not only are several of them my good friends to this day, but they have served their church as teachers, lectors, committee chairs, and volunteers of all sorts. They manifest the fruits of the Spirit that St. Paul lists in Galatians 5:22, and it is by their fruits that I know them to be of the Lord. They have enriched the life and ministry of my parishes, to say nothing of what their friendship has meant to me personally.

I feel today much as Peter must have felt after the dream recounted in Acts 10. He knew the Bible and could quote many scripture passages to prove that Gentiles were unclean. In his dream, however, a voice said to him, "What God has made clean, you must not call profane." Then Peter was approached by messengers from a Roman centurion, a man Peter's understanding of the Bible would have required him to reject as unclean. Recognizing the import of his dream, however, Peter went to the centurion, listened to his story, and said, "I truly understand that God shows no partiality." The Holy Spirit then fell upon Jew and Gentile alike, and Peter arranged for the centurion and his associates to be baptized. On biblical and other grounds, I once regarded gay and lesbian people as unclean, but having witnessed and benefited from the ministry of gay and lesbian persons, lay and ordained, I cannot call profane what God has made clean, and like Peter, I now see that "God shows no partiality."

Many have suggested that persons with a homosexual orientation remain celibate; they are not required to change their orientation, just refrain from sex. While this argument carried weight with me for a time, as I learned more about celibacy, I came to see choice as an integral part of it. Choosing a monastic or other celibate vocation is a personal decision joyfully embraced. Having it forced on someone by an outside authority violates the intention and spirit of the celibate vocation.

So if it were solely up to me, I would solemnize the union of a mature, committed same-sex couple, and if I were a bishop and it were solely up to me, I would consider for ordination a qualified, spiritually gifted gay person. Like my straight friends, my gay friends are a blessing to me. So if it were solely up to me . . .

But it's not solely up to me. Some things are more important than my personal views. I'm not in the vanguard of those pushing for the blessing of same-sex unions, partly because other social, theological, and moral questions are of greater concern to me, but mainly because of the nature of the church as a community of believers accountable to one another. I'm not in this alone, but am accountable to my brother and sister Christians for what I say and do. Moreover, the Episcopal Church in the United States is a small part of the worldwide Christian church and should honor the wisdom of the wider church.

Having spent several months among Methodists and Anglicans in two African countries, I am keenly aware of how abhorrent most African Christians — and Africa is where the Christian church is most vibrant today — find any act of homosexuality. I would never willingly or knowingly cause offense to my brothers and sisters in Africa, just as they would never willingly or knowingly cause offense to me. When the General Convention of the Episcopal Church endorsed the election of an openly gay bishop in 2003 and "recognized" that Episcopal congregations "are operating within the bounds of our common life as they explore and experience liturgies celebrating and blessing same-sex unions," I was in sympathy with the convention's actions, but Anglicans elsewhere (and more than a few U.S. Episcopalians) received the news as a betrayal, a breach of faith, and an act of arrogance or hubris. Our church appeared to think we were the only ones with the truth and that the rest of the world was ignorant and behind the times. When others perceive Americans as disdainful — and both our political and our church leaders sometimes appear that way — we lose their trust and goodwill. We Americans don't like to wait, but could we not have waited until our understanding of human sexuality was more widely shared?

But ecclesiastical controversies aside, the bottom line on gays and lesbians for me is that although I've read a good bit about human sexuality, I don't understand much about sex — straight, gay, or otherwise. Even my own sexuality often mystifies me. Where I am ignorant, I try not to draw lines that separate people. God knows what's what and who's who, and if there are lines to be drawn, let God draw them. Someday perhaps things will become clear to me. I would like that, but I don't look for it soon.

Humility

For a long time I misunderstood humility. I thought it was a somber sorrow for sin, and there were times when I strove for such a sorrow. That probably made me a grave young man, lacking the joy and freedom the great saints exhibit. Only gradually did I come to see that humility is not about sorrow but the realization that we are tiny pieces of a resplendent universe, not the center of it. Humility is the happy acceptance of one's place in the order of things. John the Baptist manifested it when he stepped aside for Jesus. The Apostle Paul manifested it when he wrote to the Philippians, "I have learned, in whatever state I am, to be content." John Wesley exhibited humility when he prayed, "I am no longer my own, but thine. Put me to what thou wilt, rank me with whom thou wilt.... Let me have all things, let me have nothing. I freely and heartily yield all things to thy pleasure and disposal." Reinhold Niebuhr showed humility in his famous prayer: "God, grant me the serenity to accept the things I cannot change, the courage to change the things I can, and the wisdom to know the difference. With this serenity, I shall live one day at a time...take, as Christ did, this imperfect world as it is and not as I would have it to be, trust that God will make all things right if I surrender to God's will."

Humility may be especially hard for clergy because the church dresses us up in regal outfits and speaks of our office in triumphalist terms. We are called "reverend," which means worthy of profound respect, and some of us are *very, right,* or *most* reverend. In some sense, we represent God. If we take that too seriously, it's hard to be humble.

I am still learning the joy of humility, but I have learned some things about it that I didn't know when I began my career.

When Pam and I arrived in Romney, West Virginia, in June 1970, I was freshly graduated from Vanderbilt Divinity School, ordained just days earlier, my mind filled with visions of grandeur. Never mind that St. Stephen's Church in Romney, where I would serve as vicar, was a congregation with an average Sunday attendance of about twenty, a number that had hardly varied for as long as anyone could remember. I had energy, vision, plans — but not much humility.

A few months later, the local Community Action Agency approached me about operating its Head Start program in the house next to the church. St. Stephen's owned the house and used it on Sundays for classroom space, but it sat vacant during the week. I thought a Head Start program would be a splendid use for the church property. The Head Start people even offered to make renovations in the house to bring it to compliance with local building codes. Although as vicar I could have given permission myself for Head Start to meet in the house, I thought it politically wise to gain the support of the vestry. The vestry discussed the proposal for two and a half hours. Arguments on both sides were presented: The building would be abused. It would be unavailable for church use during the week. We would have no control over what went on in our facilities. On the other hand, children were in need and we had a facility that could help them. We could evict Head Start if things didn't work out. We knew many of the people involved and trusted them. All twelve vestry members were present that night. Around and around we went. People began to repeat themselves and stopped listening. Positions hardened. As the evening wore on, I began to realize that if a vote were taken, it would be split evenly, six for and six against. What would I do then? I felt backed into a corner from which there was no graceful exit.

Peggy Newell was a wise and respected older member of the vestry. She had been diagnosed with terminal cancer and had almost missed the meeting because of her illness. I had seen her grow visibly exhausted as the evening progressed. Finally, Peggy said, "Why don't we pray?" Praying had not occurred to me, for I had been too busy defending my position. A moment of awkward silence followed. No one felt comfortable opposing prayer, but I expect I wasn't the only one who didn't have much confidence in it at that moment. And so we went around the table, each person asking for guidance, awkwardly and hesitantly in most cases. When the last one had prayed, someone said, "I think we can vote now." I wasn't sure about that, but everyone wanted the evening to end, so we proceeded to vote. The Head Start program was invited to meet in the church's house. The vote was eleven to one. The one dissenter stormed out of the room and said he'd never return. He had been the largest contributor to the church's operating budget, but the other eleven said they weren't going to worry about it, and the following fall, pledges were up, even without that man's participation.

I got what I wanted when the vote was taken that evening, but I hadn't done it myself and couldn't have done it myself. I had tried for over two hours to win the day through my own force of persuasion, and all I had done was polarize the vestry. I think the vote that night was my first inkling that there really is a higher power who operates, sometimes through me, sometimes around me, sometimes despite me. I also realized that when it came to spiritual maturity, I wasn't worthy to polish Peggy Newell's shoes.

A month later I had another lesson in humility. Four weeks of vacation were due to me, but with the Head Start program moving into the house next door and other initiatives planned for the fall, I felt I shouldn't be away from St. Stephen's that long. Momentum would be lost and things might fall apart. The bishop of West Virginia, Wilburn C. Campbell, was in Romney and came to call on me. Campbell raised his eyebrows, wrinkled his bald forehead, and then said to me, "There's been an Episcopal congregation here in Romney since before the Revolutionary War. Most of the families who were here then are still here now, and they'll be here in August. Now get out of here and take your vacation!" I did, and the congregation survived. It also survived a few months later when I left for good. Many small congregations, I learned, are accustomed to clergy fresh out of seminary. While they appreciate these energetic young pastors, they also know they won't stay long, so they don't take them or their fancy new ideas too seriously, even when the young pastors take themselves very seriously.

Whenever I began to think I was indispensable, that I could answer any question, that everything hung on the acceptance of my ideas, I got into trouble. You'd think, after those two experiences during the first months of my ministry, that I'd have learned to accept my place in the order of things. But it was a lesson I had to learn over and over, because having learned it, I soon forgot it. Before long, another divisive question would arise. It could be about anything — music, architecture, budgets, personnel, scheduling, doctrine — and my first instinct was to leap onto my white horse and charge off to fend for righteousness and truth. I often failed to get my way, and the church carried on much as before. Eventually I began to ask myself some questions: When everyone thinks he is contending for righteousness and truth, could it be that no one is contending for righteousness and truth? The Christian church has been muddling along fairly well for two millennia without me, so what reason is there to believe it will collapse today if denied the benefit of my wisdom? If I were suddenly removed from the scene, leaving no one to defend my point of view, could God manage?

I'd answer in the affirmative to all those questions now, and when I'm about to forget the answers, God does something to remind me of them again. It keeps me humble.

Hypocrites

"I don't come to church because there are so many hypocrites there. Why don't you people try as hard to be Christians Monday through Saturday as you do on Sunday?"

Someone actually said that to me once. I suspect lots of people think of churchgoers as hypocrites, and that may be one reason they stay away. Such thoughts are rarely expressed to me, though, probably because people who stay away from church don't want to talk with me about it, and when they do, they don't call churchgoers "hypocrites" because they think I'd argue with them or suspect they were talking about me.

It's true, of course. Churchgoers are hypocrites, all of us. When we walk through the church door on Sunday morning, looking respectable if not downright dainty, we bring our hypocrisy to church with us. Hypocrisy is a sin. Nor is it the only sin of which churchgoers are guilty. We also bring with us to church our selfishness, wobbly commitment, petty grievances, injured pride, spiritual lethargy, false values, and a sack full of other spiritual rubbish. The rubbish is part of who we are, and we could hardly show up at church, or anywhere else, without it.

Something often happens to us when we bring our rubbish to church. Jesus examines it, then takes it and lays it aside, cleans us up to make us presentable, and throws a big banquet at which we are his honored guests. All we are asked to do is to bring our rubbish. If we try to leave it at home and pretend we don't have any rubbish, then we're being dishonest with Jesus and with ourselves. We do sometimes try to do that, and that's hypocrisy. Only those who come to Jesus without pretense can get cleaned up and partake of his banquet, and in our best moments, that's what we do.

So it's true that there are hypocrites in church. It could not be otherwise. There are hypocrites outside the church as well. Hypocrites are everywhere. Everybody is a hypocrite much of the time, pretending to be holier, smarter, stronger, wealthier, sexier, or more in the know than they are. The difference between Christians and others is not that Christians are better than others or that we fancy ourselves better than others. The difference is that we know we are hypocrites, and a lot of other nasty things as well. We go to church precisely because we know what we are. The church is where sinners get cleaned up, just as a hospital is where sick people get well. Only the sick need a hospital; only sinners need a church.

As I've dealt with hypocrites over the years, both within and without the church, and reflected on my own hypocrisy, I've learned to be more accepting of others' shortcomings. C. S. Lewis said that when he began attending church and worshiping alongside other ordinary, flawed people, "my conceit just began peeling off." The same has happened to me, and the fact that I was usually to be found in the pulpit or at the altar rather than in the pew made the peeling off of my conceit all the more intense for me. As I looked out at my congregation, I saw not only hypocrites, but every other kind of sinner as well, all of them on their knees asking to be forgiven, healed, and re-created in the image of Jesus. Some of their prayers, I knew, were more heartfelt, humble, and pure than my own. I asked myself what right I had to be in the same room with those people, much less to preach to them or administer the body and blood of Christ to them. Hypocrites? The church is usually full of them, but when I show up, there's one hypocrite there for sure.

Incarceration

Only twice in my first twenty years as a priest did I enter a jail or prison. A few months after my ordination, I entered the Hampshire County jail in West Virginia as a representative of the local ministerial association. I felt ill at ease and at a loss for words. I did not make a return visit. Fifteen years later, I entered another county jail, in St. Louis, to see a member of my parish, a man who had murdered his wife. Again, I felt ill at ease and at a loss for words. I was therefore not keen on saying yes to a request in 1992 that I spend three days inside the G. K. Fountain State Correctional Facility in Atmore, Alabama. But several things gnawed at me. One was that the parishioners making the request were not asking me to visit the prison on their behalf, but that I join them there. Another was that these were some of the finest Christians I knew. And then there was that bothersome statement of Jesus about people who visited those in prison and people who didn't and what might become of them. In short, I would have felt guilty if I'd said no. I said yes — but I didn't want to go.

The event was a Kairos weekend. Designed on the popular Cursillo model, the weekend involved twenty or so men coming to the state prison to give talks and lead discussions with inmates about inviting Jesus into their lives. Inmates had to be invited by the prison chaplain to participate. Some were eager to learn about Jesus, but many just wanted a good meal. The hook was that meals for Kairos participants would be prepared by volunteers outside the prison and would feature tasty foods the prisoners hadn't seen since their incarceration.

I learned a lot in those three days. I also left the prison with new learnings and questions rumbling around in my head:

The scriptures have levels of meaning that I usually overlook. When I returned from the weekend, I resumed my usual daily Bible reading. Psalms 56 and 57 were appointed for my first day back on the outside. They contain these lines: "I live in the midst of lions that devour the people; their teeth are spears and arrows, their tongue a sharp sword.... Whenever I am afraid, I will put my trust in you." As I recalled what the inmates I met had done to their victims and the brutality and inhumanity of prison life itself, those lines took on new force for me. The Old Testament lesson for my first day back home was Nehemiah 6, a passage about the building of a wall to keep certain people out of the city of Jerusalem. How ironic, I thought, that I had just returned from a place where walls — and barbed-wire fences and guard towers — had been built to keep certain people *in.* I wondered why it was necessary to separate people from each other. Are there behaviors, attitudes, and social policies that could render walls unnecessary?

Why were there so many black people in there? About 25 percent of the residents of Alabama are black, but about 75 percent of the inmates at G. K. Fountain were black. Why? Part of the reason may have been that more crimes were committed by black people than by white people — but if that was true, why was it true? That a greater number of black children are reared in poor, one-parent households surely has something to do with it — but why was that the case? And could it be that some white judges, despite their intention to apply the law indiscriminately, impose stiffer sentences on black people because of a subtle bias against them? How much unacknowledged prejudice lurks in white hearts, including my own?

There but for the grace of God go I. All the prisoners I met were poorly educated, as evidenced by their grammar, vocabulary, and lack of the kind of knowledge books provide. One inmate, a young man whom I especially liked, was named John Wesley Rhymes. "How wonderful that you have been named for such a great Christian," I said. His blank look told me he had never heard of the eighteenth century's greatest Christian witness. I told him about John Wesley, of his conversion experience, his evangelical passion, his preaching in the fields and streets, his journal and prayers. When I returned home, I mailed John Wesley Rhymes copies of passages from John Wesley's writings that I thought he'd like. How could this young Christian never have heard of his great namesake? The obvious answer was that no one had told him. How fortunate — should I say favored? lucky? blessed? — I am to have been born to parents who not only gave me a set of values, but also inspired me to read and learn. My good education has opened doors for me and enlarged my sense of the power and goodness of God. Had I been born to other parents, might I today be sleeping in a bunk above John Wesley Rhymes at the G. K. Fountain State Correctional Facility?

Many things are less important than I think; a few are more important. Seeing someone break into tears at the simplest expression of affection or affirmation — one inmate told me he had been in the state prison system for twenty years and until that weekend had never received a letter, phone call, gift, or visit from the outside — made me ashamed of the emphasis I often place on things that don't matter as much as a single visit to a lonely or bereft person. It makes buying yet another sweater, book, or compact disc for myself seem almost shameful, and ecclesiastical squabbles over doctrine, budgets, and liturgical niceties seem silly.

Ministering together in the Lord's name melts differences. At the table where I was assigned were six inmates and three visitors — a Pentecostal layman, an Episcopal layman, and me. I never learned the Episcopal layman's views, but I quickly realized that the Pentecostal layman was several light-years to the right of me on most of the issues modern Christians bicker about. He probably knew it, too. But it didn't matter to either of us. We weren't there to iron out theological and moral wrinkles, but to witness to the love of Christ for the lost. As we listened to the inmates' stories, we tried to model that love. How astonishing, I thought, that when Christians model the love of Christ, differences fade into the background. Could one of the problems with the modern church be that we put most of our energy into things other than modeling the love of Christ?

Significant as that weekend was for me, it was overshadowed by what came next. Some time later, one of the laymen who had asked me to take part in the Kairos weekend came to see me again. I knew he and two other men from St. Paul's Church had been driving to the prison once a week for three years to take part in a small Bible study and prayer group with some of the inmates. He said to me, "We need your help, Dick. We've always made a point not to talk much about ourselves when we're on the inside, but to listen to the men. We never mentioned what church we came from, didn't think it mattered. But some of the men asked us about our church, so we told them we were Episcopalians. They wanted to know what that meant, so we told them what we knew. Then they asked about baptism and about communion. They wanted to know our doctrine, how we interpret the Bible. They asked about church government and authority. So we got them a Prayer Book and some other literature. But they still have questions. Finally, we said, 'You need to talk to our priest.' So we're asking you, Dick, will you go up there and meet with these men?"

By then I had served on a second Kairos weekend and was no longer uncomfortable at the thought of entering a prison, so I readily agreed — and I was humbled by the prisoners I met. Here were men who had presumably done something awful (I later found out what some of them had done, and it was indeed awful) and who lived under circumstances too grim for me to imagine. Prison life is fraught with risks, to both body and soul. The gospel is mocked there. People are attacked and stabbed there. Manipulative, abusive sex is common in the dormitories. Any sign of need, loneliness, or sorrow may be met with laughter and scorn. Most prisoners maintain an outward show of bravado, however frightened or discouraged they may be inside. I can think of few places less conducive to living one's life at the side of Jesus. But the men I met at the prison that afternoon had pored over the scriptures and the Book of Common Prayer and asked thoughtful questions about what they had found there. They asked for things to read on church history and doctrine. They prayed with and for me. They told me how they appreciated my visit, which reassured them that the church on the outside had not forgotten them.

I was unable to deal with all their questions that day, so I agreed to return. Three weeks later, they had read what I had given them on my first visit and now asked for more reading. I began to visit the prison frequently. We were fortunate in gaining the services of Rus Ford, a retired priest and former Illinois state patrolman who had retired in Alabama. Rus was able to relate to the men better than I could, and he went to the facility twice a week. He began to celebrate a weekly Eucharist in the prison chapel. Eventually, Bishop Charles Duvall began making visitations to the prison. He confirmed twenty-two inmates the first year. One of the inmates said to the bishop, "If we're going to be Episcopalians, shouldn't we belong to a parish?" The bishop said that would normally be the case, but there was no organized parish inside the prison. The inmate then turned to me and asked whether he could become a member of St. Paul's in Daphne. Later that week, I added to the roll of St. Paul's Church his name and those of three other inmates whose residences on the outside were near Daphne. They kept up with parish life through the weekly newsletter, occasional visits and gifts from parishioners, and by praying for members of the parish. When I visited them, they asked me about people on the parish prayer list. One inmate constructed a detailed model of St. Paul's Church from photographs, which he gave to the parish.

We contacted Episcopal congregations in the hometowns of other inmates, and some of the inmates began corresponding with members of parishes near their homes. A few became members of their home-town Episcopal congregations. They would say things to me like, "I got a letter from St. Philip's Church in my hometown today! And I know where that church is — it's that stone church on Sycamore Street. I never knew that was an *Episcopal* church." I suspected most of them had never heard of the Episcopal Church before entering prison, much less known where the nearest parish was.

By the time I left Alabama in August 2000, the Episcopal community within the prison had grown to the point where a congregation had been organized. They call themselves the St. Dismas Fellowship — named for the penitent thief who was crucified with Jesus — and they evangelize their brothers within the prison walls. St. Dismas has its own newsletter and Web site. All is not perfect at St. Dismas, any more than all is perfect at a parish on the outside. There are instances of backsliding, token commitment, and hypocrisy. But there are also unmistakable instances of lives changed, lost souls being found, the spiritually dead being raised to life again. I still pray daily for several of the inmates to whom I have grown close, and whenever I return to Alabama to visit friends, I always take a day to visit my friends at the G. K. Fountain State Correctional Facility in Atmore. Of all the blessings that my thirty years of ministry brought to me, none was more unexpected than the blessing of knowing these men and sharing the love of Christ with them.

_____ **Jack-of-All-Trades**

I remember my youth as a time of boundless idealism, enthusiasm, drive, and ambition. Like most young people, I gave hardly a thought to the possibility of illness, disability, or failure. No goal was beyond my reach. I wouldn't have said the sky was my limit because that would have been to acknowledge a limit. Of course I recognized, in theory, that as a human being I was constrained by the bounds of time and space, but in day-to-day practice I took little account of bounds. This attitude, typical of many young people, results in achievements that we older people would not trouble ourselves to attempt. The energy and idealism of youth are marvelous things.

But youth is also naive, and when things don't work out for us as we had hoped, we have two alternatives: we can become cynical and give up trying to do anything, or we can become wise and more realistic in what we undertake. I think I became wise and more realistic.

Certainly I was not the only young clergyman who began his career with starry-eyed dreams of his future in the church. While the energy in those dreams was often a blessing to me and the parishes I served, hindsight shows me that the dreams were also a hidden trap — into which I fell headlong. Perhaps the naiveté of youth is most pronounced in the helping professions, but in one respect, a pastor is set up for disillusionment in a way that few others are, even in other helping professions. While professions such as medicine and law have moved toward specialization, the pastor is still a generalist. We see ourselves (and are often seen by others) as ecclesiastical jacks-of-all-trades. We charge forward to preach, teach, pray, write, administer, talk, listen, comfort, challenge, motivate, mediate, hire, fire, and sometimes mop the floors and shovel the snow. We will be all things to all people. But it won't work. Even if there were an infinite number of hours in every day, nobody can be all things to all people. Those who think they can do everything — as many young clergy do — soon stumble over their egos and ambitions. Invariably, we realize that we cannot create the perfect parish, please everyone, run every program, and meet every expectation. It is at that point that many a pastor leaves parish ministry to pursue some other line of work.

The alternative is to grow wiser and more realistic by recognizing our limitations and turning them to our advantage. When I accepted the call to St. Paul's, Daphne, I had been around the block enough times that I knew what I could do and what I could not do. I identified four specific tasks of ministry that I do well — preaching, writing, teaching adults, and dealing with people one-on-one and in small groups. Not surprisingly, they were also the tasks I most enjoyed. I concentrated my time and energy on those tasks. Other things — organizing projects, planning liturgies, poring over financial statements, monitoring the physical plant, making long-range projections — were not less important, but I realized I wasn't the one to do them. I either found others to do them (often they were delighted to be invited to use their gifts) or accepted the fact that some things wouldn't get done.

That was an important learning for me: some things wouldn't get done, and it would be okay. The earth would still rotate on its axis once every twenty-four hours and travel around the sun once every year. Things would perk along more or less satisfactorily, no matter what I did or didn't do. I could make a difference, in certain areas at least, but I wasn't going to transform my parish, much less the world. That realization was liberating for me. It freed me to do what I enjoy doing, find others to do the rest, and then enjoy the ride. Jack-of-all-trades? Absolutely not. Not me, not anyone. I think my realization that I couldn't do everything and shouldn't try to has been one reason that the second half of my adult life has been so much happier and more serene than the first half. Growing old, if you've learned something along the way, has its charms.

Kids

During the two years I was out of parish ministry in the 1980s, I learned some things I might never have learned hovering around the altar. One thing I learned was to let noisy children be. Don't reprove them or their parents, however much they may be disturbing your serenity. Others may be annoyed by the noise, but when you're running the show, you are annoyed the most because you're the one competing with the children for the congregation's attention. Also, parents are embarrassed when attention is called to their unruly children, and a pastor doesn't endear himself to parents by embarrassing them. But the main reason to let the children be is what that willingness says about our understanding of God.

The parish where my family and I worshiped for those two years was a small neighborhood church on a back street, St. Philip's-in-the-Fields, in Oreland, Pennsylvania. One Sunday St. Philip's held one of those multiple baptisms that have become so popular in recent years. Upon entering the church that day, I headed for my usual seat in the front. When I'm in the congregation, I like to sit up front where there's usually lots of room and I can stretch out my lanky frame and scatter my overcoat, Prayer Book, hymnal, and bulletin two or three feet in all directions without fear of invading anyone else's space.

That day, however, my pew and those near it were filled with strangers who didn't know what was going on. That was fine with me. People who didn't know what was going on were wise to sit where they could see our rector, Jack Jessup. Jack used body language and facial expressions to give out little signals about what to do.

The four infants being baptized that morning all had more brothers and sisters than is common in Episcopal families. Judging from their numbers, I'd say they were born at nine-month intervals. And that was to say nothing of their cousins, not one of whom was missing that morning. I sat as close to the front as I could. This placed me within whispering distance of enough infants and toddlers to populate a nursery school, but I never found out how many of them were actually within whispering distance because none of them whispered.

The baptisms went reasonably well, and when I grew tired of trying to see over the heads of the crowd of parents and godparents in front of me, I entertained myself by winking at a winsome toddler in the next pew who was celebrating the holy occasion by dropping her rattle on the floor and watching her mommy pick it up and glare at her. I finally gave her my bulletin to chew.

The problem came during the Eucharistic prayer, by which time the infant population had grown weary of worship. Adults who grow weary of worship simply start daydreaming and no one is the wiser. Not so with infants. Four or five of them began a stream-of-consciousness commentary on how they felt about being there. The church lacked carpeting and pew cushions, which made for sharp acoustics when the organ was playing. The acoustics worked equally well when infants were screaming.

I found out one doesn't actually have to hear the Eucharistic prayer to follow it if one is familiar with the Prayer Book. I had an idea of what Jack was probably saying at the altar as the prayer unfolded. I like to cross myself at the part about the sanctification of the worshipers, and I probably wasn't more than a few words ahead or behind with my gesturing, though I couldn't say for sure, the noise being what it was.

At first I was irritated at the cacophony. *Why don't those parents remove those children?* I thought. But then I remembered Mark 10:14: "Let the little children come to me, do not hinder them; for to such belongs the kingdom of God." I'd always imagined those children whom Jesus welcomed as pretty little girls in pigtails and respectful little boys whose mothers had just combed their hair — cute, courteous, adorable. But what if they weren't like that? What if they were bickering, spitting on each other, calling each other nasty names, ignoring parental discipline, and screaming, "That's mine!" What if that's precisely why the disciples sought to keep the kids away from Jesus? What if, when Jesus said to let the little children come, he was speaking of insufferable brats?

Then I thought about myself. Maybe that's how God feels about me. When I besiege God with my prayers, maybe God says, "Here comes Schmidt with his God-awful bleating again. That guy leaves me no peace and quiet in which to meditate on my divine majesty. I sometimes think I'll have him removed. But, for all his complaining and nagging, I still love him. I guess I'll put up with him. So let the little brat come, for to such belongs my kingdom."

So I say let the kids stay, noise and all. What better way to model godly behavior for them?

_____ **Lost and Found**

I always enjoyed playing softball in the church league. I played up through my mid-fifties, until my bones told me one day that they no longer enjoyed sliding into second base. Since I'm tall and lanky, I usually played first base, but my favorite position was left field, where I could chase long fly balls and occasionally leap to catch one. Once in West Virginia, I leapt off the side of a mountain and tumbled down a rocky ravine, but I caught the ball and held onto it. It was worth the bruises.

I usually removed my wedding ring and placed it in my pants pocket when I stepped to the plate, because it could wear a blister on my finger when I swung the bat. One evening, after having returned home from a game in Alabama, I discovered my ring wasn't in my pants pocket. I searched every room of the house; I searched my car; I returned to the ball field and raked the dirt around home plate, first base, and the dugout. No wedding ring. The next day, I telephoned the local police, pawn shops, and the Fairhope Recreation Department. I posted notices at the field. As days passed and no one telephoned, my hopes of finding my wedding ring waned.

It felt like grief. The ring was a valuable piece of jewelry, but its monetary value had nothing to do with my sense of loss. I recalled the day twenty-four years earlier when Pam and I had selected our rings at a jewelry store in downtown Louisville. I recalled the moment she slipped the ring onto my finger as we exchanged our wedding vows.

97

I remembered the ring's inscription, with both of our initials and the date of our wedding. I felt almost as if I had lost Pam herself.

But of course I hadn't lost her. I still had what really mattered. The ring was important to me only because it symbolized our commitment to each other, a commitment that continued with or without the ring. Reflecting on the loss of my wedding ring, I was reminded of my feelings about the Holy Eucharist. One of the reasons I like being an Episcopalian is that I want to receive the body and blood of Christ each week. How would I feel if I were unable to receive the sacrament? Grief would be a good word for it, a grief like what I felt when I lost my wedding ring. But I also know the Eucharist is not essential. Christ's commitment to me and mine to Christ are signified by the sacrament, but they do not depend on it.

The loss of my ring also taught me how kind people can be. The day after I lost my ring I called Ray and Shirley Walley, parishioners whom I had liked but did not know well. I did know, though, that they owned a metal detector. Could I borrow it to search the ball field more meticulously? No, they said, because using the equipment required training and experience — but they would be happy to search the field for me. The next day I met Shirley at the ball field at 7:00 a.m. The south Alabama heat and humidity were already grim at that hour, but we searched the field foot by foot for an hour and a half. Still no wedding ring. I asked myself: *Would I have given so much of my time in that heat to help someone else search for a ring? Maybe*, I thought, but I wasn't sure. I was glad, though, to be part of a church where people care that much.

The story has a happy ending. A week after I lost my ring, Pam noticed a gold glimmer on the floor next to one of the casters beneath our bed. It was the missing ring! It must have slipped out of my pants pocket and rolled beneath the caster where it was hard to see.

"I wasn't worried. I knew you'd find your ring because I was praying every day that you would," my assistant priest told me the next day. *Well, you never know about that,* I thought. There are always two explanations for happy events. Some people speak of coincidence and good luck; other people speak of prayer and the hand of God. All I knew was that I was overjoyed at finding my ring and that its loss had revealed to me how much I loved Pam and how much my parishioners loved me. Somewhere in all that, God was at work, and I thanked God for it.

$\mathcal{M}$ _____ Marriage I

I began to enjoy weddings when I learned to regard them as theater. I don't take theater all that seriously, and I don't take weddings as seriously as most people do. The most contrived and artificial gathering I know of is the New Year's Eve party. It celebrates the changing of a calendar on the wall when everyone knows things will be pretty much the same the next day except for the incidence of headaches. Many weddings have something of that unreal quality to them because it's not the wedding that matters — it's the marriage, though few people are thinking about that. Getting married matters, but only because of the lifelong union those promises set up. How the wedding is done is not important — but how the couple manages the tensions and family pressures that usually surface in the months before a wedding can tell them a lot about what to expect of one another down the line.

In premarital instructions with engaged couples, I always encouraged them to look beyond the wedding, which would last forty-five minutes at most, to what would follow, perhaps several decades of living together as husband and wife. That meant reflecting on their different personalities and temperaments, family backgrounds, role expectations, ways of managing money, religious priorities, sex, children, in-laws, and all the rest of it. Engaged couples were willing to talk with me about such things (perhaps because I required it), and I trust our conversations did some good for at least some of them. But often their energy, especially the bride's, was in planning every detail of those forty-five minutes at the church.

Marrying Pam was the best thing I ever did, and not for one moment have I regretted marrying her. We have had a good marriage for thirty-six years — but our marriage has not been one of seamless happiness. No marriage is. Marriages would be better, I believe, if wives and husbands entered into them with a clearer understanding of what love is. It's not the same as romantic involvement (although that's present in a good marriage, too). Romantic passion is a state of heightened energy, focused on another person. You cannot, in fact, *not* think about the other person when swept up in romantic passion. It is exhilarating and thrilling, but it can also captivate you (that is, imprison you), and it can consume you (that is, devour you). People caught in this sort of involvement aren't in love — they're *crazy* about each other, and that is the right word. Romantic involvement is exhausting, even debilitating. Because it relies on excitement, it's also self-centered (although it appears to be other-centered). Hollywood and commercial advertisers revel in romance, as if it were the same as love — and if we take their word as gospel, we will invariably be disappointed in marriage. Although healthy romance is a happy feature of most good marriages, romantic involvement cannot endure at peak intensity. Like the tide, it comes and goes, and this in-and-outness is one of the marks of a healthy marriage.

Marriage is about love, not romance. The best definition of love I know of is found in the marriage vow itself: "I, John, take you, Mary, to be my wife, to have and to hold from this day forward, for better for worse, for richer for poorer, in sickness and in health, to love and to cherish, until we are parted by death." Those words make no reference to romance. Weddings are about romance — flowers, pretty dresses, invitations, and photographs to record the ultimate romantic moment. Marriage is something different.

A marriage is a living, growing thing, nurtured by love and sometimes beset by the world. For example, most married people occasionally experience romantic interest in persons other than their mates. Such feelings are normal and they fade in time; they are not to be taken seriously. What is to be taken seriously is words like these: "I'll be there for you until I die, whether I feel like it or not, whether it's fun or not, whether it's easy or not, whether I like you or not, whether you deserve it or not. You can count on me as long as there is breath in me. I will never leave you." *That* is love. Love is not about romance; it is about commitment.

I do not mean to make marriage sound like a burden. On the contrary, I know of no greater joy in this life than that which comes from making such a commitment. When two people promise to love and cherish each other as long as they live, and really mean it, a deep confidence and peace come to the soul. It is rather like knowing and responding to the love of God, which is why so many of the great saints write of their faith in words that sound erotic. It is also why the Prayer Book says Christian marriage "signifies to us the mystical union between Christ and his church." People know that weddings have something to do with love, but they get carried away with the ceremony and the reception and forget what love is. Love is "I will never forsake you." God was the first to say it, and when we hear that promise, it is our highest joy to respond, "Nor will we forsake you." The Bible is the story of the unfolding relationship between God and his people. It is the original love story.

 **Marriage II**

The strangest letter I ever received arrived in the mail one day in 1991. It was unsigned, but the author made it clear that she knew me, quoting things I had said from the pulpit. She said she loved her husband but that there was little romance in their marriage. She was considering whether to enter into a sexual relationship with another man and wanted to know what I thought about it. She asked that I respond to a post office box. Fortunately, this letter arrived after I'd been married for over two decades and had learned some things about commitment. It was not difficult to know how to respond. I was able to respond with candor and honesty:

Dear friend,

You might be surprised at how familiar your predicament is to me. Not only have I heard others express similar feelings, but Pam and I have experienced such feelings from time to time. I suppose that sooner or later, most married people must make the decision you now face.

I was not surprised to read that you and John feel "like two little kids" and "so free and unburdened" when you are together. That's usually the case when two people who are not married to each other find themselves drawn to one another, and it is perhaps especially so for you and John since you say you usually meet at an out-of-the-way restaurant and then walk along the beach together. People who are courting (that's the best term for your relationship with John) don't have to deal with balancing the checkbook, hair in curlers, demanding children, daily exposure to unpleasant character traits, unbrushed teeth in the morning, unwashed dishes stacked in the kitchen, dirty socks on the floor, and times when you want to stay up and he wants to go to bed, you want to eat out and he wants to eat in, you want to spend and he wants to save, you want to leave a party and he wants to stay, or any of the thousands of other disagreements which confront husbands and wives daily.

Marriage, on the other hand, includes all these things. Wives and husbands come to know each other far more intimately and fully than people who are courting. Marriage is deep; courtship is superficial. Marriage partners learn to compromise, forgive, and accept one another in full knowledge of the other's weaknesses and failures. Each is there for the other, regardless of circumstances. Feelings and moods come and go, but the marriage remains because it is stronger than feelings and moods.

This kind of commitment is called love. It produces spiritual maturity, and the Bible says the love of God for his people is like the love of husband and wife. This maturity does not come from courtship. Courtship, whether or not either of the parties is already married to someone else, is more fun than marriage, but fun is what it is — not love. Marriage, because it includes commitment and love, can last a lifetime. Courtship is by its nature transient.

You asked me whether God would punish you if you had an affair with John. I can only give you my opinion, since the grace and judgment of God are mysteries which I have experienced but do not fully understand. I don't believe God punishes us. That is, God does not sit in heaven with a giant mallet and say, "If you offend, I'll bash you." I do believe, though, that God grieves when we depart from his ways, and I believe you will be punished if you have sex with John. But the punishment will arise out of the nature of infidelity itself. It will begin with the sense of guilt you will feel when you look at yourself in the mirror. It could also include the pain of divorce and/or disillusionment when (1) the bloom of your affair with John wears off, or (2) you discover that John does not want to marry you or you do not want to marry him, or (3) you marry John and find dealing with him day to day in marriage a far different thing from seeing him occasionally in carefully chosen romantic settings.

Except in cases of abuse, I feel it is better to work on a marriage than to risk losing it. And entering into an extramarital affair invites that risk. You said in your letter that you love your husband even as you are drawn to John. That love is a gift from God to you and your husband. I hope you will thank God for it and think long before you jeopardize it.

$\mathcal{M}$ _____ **Monasticism**

During my Presbyterian childhood, I gave hardly a thought to monks and nuns. No monastics lived in Shelbyville, Kentucky, and if I thought of them at all, I envisioned spooky, medieval creatures shuffling through dark passageways. I had never meet a monastic, but I did when I went to college. Kenyon College was an all-male institution in the 1960s, and from time to time a bus full of coeds from an all-female school would be brought to campus for a dance. Such a group had arrived from a Roman Catholic school in Pittsburgh in February of my freshman year, chaperoned by an imposing elderly nun dressed in head-to-toe black habit. She reminded me of a commandant.

As a card-carrying, flag-waving Protestant just tasting academic theology for the first time, I thought I should take my stand, so I said to her, "You know, ma'am, I think Luther was right." I wasn't sure "ma'am" was the right way to address a nun, but it was the only thing I knew to say. I was expecting her to respond with some feeble defense of papist superstition, to which I would quote scripture, and we could do the Reformation all over again, right there on a dance floor in Knox County, Ohio. I felt pretty sure of myself. But the nun looked at me and replied, "Of course Luther was right." Her expression seemed to add, "Doesn't everyone know that?" I mumbled something and slunk away. Clearly, I had nothing to say that she hadn't heard before.

In later years, I climbed down from my high horse and discovered I had much to learn from monastics. In the early 1970s, I spent three days at an Episcopal monastery in upstate New York on a directed silent retreat. It was the first time I had ever intentionally observed a time of silence, and I found it exhilarating. Later on, I made silent retreats at other monasteries, both Episcopal and Roman. Spending time under direction in a monastic setting helped me when I was seeking guidance in times of uncertainty or when I simply wanted to listen to God. I was also in spiritual direction for two years under a nun of the Cenacle Sisters, and I studied at a Jesuit school, Spring Hill College in Mobile, Alabama, where I enjoyed friendships among the priests who ran the place. An Episcopal order, the Community of Celebration, visited my parish in Alabama and led a splendid workshop on church music. By the time I retired, I had come full circle in my thoughts about monks and nuns. I now see them as among the most perceptive and savvy people anywhere.

Monastic orders differ, both in the Episcopal and in the Roman Catholic churches. Most, however, adhere to some version of the threefold vow of poverty, chastity, and obedience, which is to say, monks and nuns promise not to seek money, sex, or power. Modern Western culture is based on the drive to acquire precisely those three things; just look at an evening's ads on television and ask what is being used to sell everything from automobiles to orange juice. For much of my life I have obsessed about one or another of those three things. As I have spent time in monastic houses and gotten to know several nuns and monks well, I have come to see the monastic vows of poverty, chastity, and obedience not as confining, but as liberating. Most people could learn a lot from a week in a monastery.

People in religious orders forego the privilege of owning private property in order to be free from its encumbrances. Destitution and physical pain are not monastic virtues (although this has not always been understood). All the monastic houses I have visited served nutritious and tasty meals, and the brothers and sisters lived simply but comfortably, listening to music and watching television just like the rest of us. But monks and nuns do not accumulate things. By contrast, we on the outside tend to accumulate as much as possible, then clutch it to ourselves until we die so that our children can then clutch it to themselves. As a result of my experiences in the cloister, I have in recent years simplified my life.

Chastity is also a liberating virtue. Men and women in the cloister are just as virile and sensual as anyone else, nor do they regard sex as sinful or nasty. But they forego sexual relations that they may be free to pursue an even more intimate and happy relationship, that between God and his creatures. Elsewhere, however, people today regard "good sex" as both a basic entitlement and one of humanity's ultimate achievements. Anyone who turns away from such pursuits is often thought to be engaged in the emotionally unhealthy practice of "repressing" natural instincts.

Obedience to God, lived out day-to-day as obedience to one's supe-rior, is intended to bring inner freedom, the freedom to become what we long to be, to realize the potential God has planted within us. It frees us to be ourselves because we no longer fret about whether we can get our way. But getting one's way is an obsession for many people outside the cloister. Our unwillingness to surrender control leads to spiritual deprivation.

Enslavement to money, sex, and power extends beyond individuals. Parishes can be enslaved as well. Parishes are enslaved to money when a new member is welcomed because she brings a new pledge rather than because she is a soul coming to Christ, when the budget drives ministry and mission, when vestries try to hold onto monetary gifts rather than use them in Christ's service. Parishes are enslaved to sex when in searching for a pastor they give preference to candidates who are tall and handsome (and male), when the presence of gay people in the church evokes polarizing rancor, when looking good on Sunday is more important than praying well. Parishes are enslaved to power when they measure their success against how well a neighboring parish is doing rather than against their own sense of mission, when differences of opinion result in winners and losers, when the parish forgets that all power is ultimately God's and that we are all powerless before him.

I have no doubt that such things occur in monasteries as well. Monks and nuns, after all, are sinners, too. There is no sin outside the cloister walls that cannot also be found within them. But on the whole, monastics are more intentional than those of us on the outside about ordering their lives according to Christian norms and, when they fall short, confessing their sins and making amends. That makes most monasteries and convents spiritually healthy places, "functional" rather than "dysfunctional," to use the current buzzwords.

I shall never forget something I heard on the radio a few years ago. The reporter was speaking of a new tax in Britain, to be paid by everyone "except for certain categories of people, such as monks, nuns, and mental patients." *What a curious threesome,* I thought. Could the British government regard monks and nuns as crazy? Have we reached a point where what has represented the highest level of spirituality to most of the Western world for most of its history is now dismissed as a form of lunacy? Certainly there are crazy people these days who are not in mental institutions, but if you want to find them, don't look in the monasteries.

$\mathcal{M}$ _____ Money

Parishes have personalities, and they are more than the sum total of the personalities of the individual parishioners. A parish's personality is determined, among other things, by its history, the clergy who have served it in the past, the community in which it is located, even its architecture. Part of a parish's personality is its attitude toward money. I've served in poor parishes and wealthy parishes, and the attitude toward money is not a function of how much money people have. In some vestries, money is the dominant topic at every meeting — not enough of it, don't spend endowment principal, trim expenses, seek more money from sources other than parishioners' pockets, and above all, don't mention tithing! Some vestries seem to think talking about money is their reason for being, and they spend so much time wrangling over the budget that they have no energy left for evangelism, prayer, or outreach. The most effective vestry I ever worked with was one where each meeting began with supper, which built collegial relationships among vestry members, and was followed by a twenty-minute Bible reflection and prayer time, which set the tone for the evening. Then, when the business session began, the monthly balance sheet was presented and dispatched within fifteen minutes, and the rest of the meeting was devoted to ministry and mission.

I have seen in more than one parish — and in my own soul — the corrosive effect of money, and I think I understand what Jesus meant when he warned that the possession of wealth was a dangerous thing. Jesus' many warnings about money gnawed at me. At times during my years in ministry I felt that people I loved were living dangerously, and, even more frightening, that I myself was living dangerously, and it had come about so subtly and gradually that I hardly knew it was happening.

As I prayed about money and my relationship to it, I came to see that the danger posed by having money consists in two things. First, money seduces. Its glamor is like that of an illicit lover whom we meet only in swank hotel rooms. We begin to think such a relationship is deep and real when really we are drawn only by the lure of glitzy surroundings and pleasure without commitment. The relationship is an empty one, but by the time we see the truth, we may have lost the relationship that really matters, with the faithful lover who would stand beside us no matter what. It is no coincidence that sexual infidelity is a common image for religious backsliding in the Bible. Eventually I was no longer surprised to meet wealthy people who were unhappy. They had been seduced. This can be true of entire parishes.

Second, money separates people. It enables them to restrict their circle, to associate only with their own kind, isolating themselves in houses set back from the road, driving through poor neighborhoods on elevated freeways with the windows rolled up. This was apparently the relationship of the rich man and Lazarus in Jesus' parable. When some people hold onto large sums while others have little or nothing, the reasons given by the well-to-do for keeping their money sound hollow. The most affluent parish I served was St. Peter's, Ladue, and the people of St. Peter's made a major step away from such isolation and toward involvement during my time there by founding, financing, and staffing a home for unwed pregnant women from the streets of inner-city St. Louis. It was a hands-on project for the people of St. Peter's, some of whom had never set foot in the part of town where the home was located.

Many poor people have better giving records than wealthy people. I remember one Every Member Canvass chairman in a parish I served, a physician who had just bought a new top-of-the-line automobile and installed a large indoor swimming pool and spa at his home, saying to me, "I think it's unrealistic in this day and age to expect anyone to tithe." I thought to myself (though I did not say it), *I tithe on a fraction of your income, and you have just bought a new car and a new spa for your home. How can you say that?* It occurred to me that "this day and age" was no different from any other and that Americans in general have a problem with our relationship to money. I never served in a parish where the highest pledge came from among the wealthiest members. It usually came from a schoolteacher, a woman who owned a small business, or a salesman.

Reflecting on my feelings about the wealthy physician who regarded tithing as unrealistic also caused me to recognize that my judgmental attitude toward him could become a problem for me, whether or not his relationship to money was a problem for him. Something was wrong in *my* soul. What my parishioners did was beyond my control. Judgmental attitudes on my part, however, were not beyond my control. If I allowed my soul to marinate in self-righteousness, it would sap my strength and isolate me from the very parishioners I loved and among whom I was called to minister. The effect would be spiritually toxic, more corrosive to my soul than affluence itself. But before I could ask God to remove that cancer from my heart, I had to recognize it and repent of it, and I found that hard to do.

$\mathcal{N}$ _____ Numbers I

Some people thrive on statistics while others make fun of them. All the parishes I served talked about numbers. I think it's true that you can "prove" just about anything if you know how to use (or misuse) statistics.

For example, average Sunday attendance at all services at St. Peter's, Ladue, rose by 10 percent in 1984, from 255 at the beginning of the year to 281 at the end of the year. Most of the new worshipers in 1984 were young adults, including several recently divorced working mothers with small children. Attendance leveled off and remained stable in 1985. The number of pledges received by St. Peter's in the fall of 1984 (for the year 1985) was 315; the number received in the fall of 1985 (for the year 1986) was 383, an increase of 22 percent. The total amount pledged for the year 1985 was $259,000; the amount pledged for 1986 was $283,000, an increase of 10 percent. The average pledge for 1986 at St. Peter's dropped to $738, from an average pledge of $822 for 1985.

What would you make of those numbers? Here's what I made of them: St. Peter's was growing, but sporadically and slowly. People who began worshiping at St. Peter's in 1984 pledged for the first time in the fall of 1985, and because they were not as financially secure as older members, new pledges that year were lower on the whole than pledges from older members.

That, I think, is a reasonable interpretation of the numbers, but others drew different conclusions from the same numbers. One vestry-man pointed to the lack of growth in attendance in 1985 to say the parish was foundering. Another pointed to the jump in the number of pledges to say the parish was flourishing. One parishioner said we were "attracting the wrong kind of people," but another said how pleased she was that people "outside the country club set" were finally discovering St. Peter's. As rector, I was both credited and blamed for what was happening.

During my six years at St. Peter's, we unwittingly fell into a trap that I call the game of "Comparison." I played this game myself without knowing it, and probably encouraged others to play it. The rules of the game are simple: compare yourself to someone else and pin your opinion of yourself on the results of the comparison.

The comparison can work in two ways, seemingly opposite but producing similar results. Some people compare themselves favorably to others, like the Pharisee who prayed, "God, I thank thee that I am not like other men, extortioners, unjust, adulterers, or even like this tax collector." The idea that we — Americans, Episcopalians, white people, Southerners, educated people, straight people, law-abiding people, men, women, whatever — are better than others leads to a smug self-righteousness. We then grow isolated from other people and become unhappy. This causes us to heap abuse on those who differ from us.

But that is not how we played the game at St. Peter's. The other way the comparison can work is to think other people are better than we are and to repeat demeaning messages to ourselves. These messages may have originated from parents, teachers, or others who influenced us during our childhood, but it doesn't matter where the messages come from. The important thing is that we still repeat them. Someone else is more beautiful, better educated, more articulate, healthier, wealthier, living in a larger home, more happily married, or in possession of some other thing that we lack but crave. When we play the game this way, we begin to resent those who have what we want. The result of this comparison is the same as with the other one: we grow isolated from other people and become unhappy. This was the way the game was played at St. Peter's during my time there.

St. Peter's and the Church of St. Michael and St. George, another Episcopal parish located nearby, were at that time the two largest congregations in the diocese. Both drew their members from the same neighborhoods, and parishioners of the two congregations worked and socialized together during the week. A friendly rivalry had developed between the two parishes, and there had long been some shifting of membership back and forth between the two.

The wind was blowing in the direction of St. Michael's during my time at St. Peter's. Two or three households each year, sometimes more, transferred from St. Peter's to St. Michael's. Although the raw numbers were not great, the impact on morale was significant, because those who left included some of St. Peter's most visible, wealthy, and well-connected people. It began to feel as if the parish was hemorrhaging. Saturday night cocktail parties became difficult for St. Peter's people. They told me they felt defensive when they discussed church with friends from St. Michael's. On one occasion, at a large social function where I was dressed in a sport coat and necktie, I began conversing with a woman I did not know. She mentioned that she worshiped at St. Michael's. I said, "I'm an Episcopalian, too. I go to St. Peter's." She responded, "Well, come over to St. Michael's and experience a *real* Episcopal church!" I said I was happy where I was and walked away feeling angry. I then knew how my parishioners felt, and I wanted us to circle the wagons to protect ourselves from such predators.

Some of my parishioners wanted to remodel our parish after St. Michael's. I commented to the vestry that the Christian church is like a bracelet and its congregations like charms on the bracelet — the appeal of the bracelet is that each charm is unique; comparison is silly and pointless. God, I said, is glorified in the diversity of his creation. No two creatures are entirely alike. To praise God rightly, we first accept ourselves and every other created being — including the church down the road — as we are, as God has seen fit to make us. God endowed each of us with gifts that are ours alone. It is not our place to judge God's handiwork; we neither lord it over those who lack our gifts nor envy those with gifts denied to us. Contentment and acceptance of all things — all persons, all creatures, all congregations — is the mark of faithfulness. It starts with acceptance of self. That's what I said, but it's not what I practiced, because I too became caught up in the "Comparison" game. I began to think in terms of winning and losing, and that's when I realized I was in trouble. I was devoted to the people of St. Peter's and committed to my work among them, but with that frame of mind, I often did not provide the leadership my parish needed.

$\mathcal{N}$ ———————— Numbers II

I had it both ways. Fairmont, West Virginia, was a former coal mining town, but most of the mines had shut down years before I arrived. People were moving out of town and there was a sense of bygone glory about the place. Our one wealthy parishioner pledged generously, but the parish budget reflected the fact that most parishioners barely made ends meet. Like some of the parishioners, Christ Church lived hand-to-mouth; it felt as if we were holding our fingers in a dike. During my seven years as rector, the parish struggled every year to pay the bills and make needed repairs to the aging church property. Christ Church experienced the same financial strains month after month, year after year. We talked a lot about finances: Would we be able to pay the light bill this month? Did we have to buy new Sunday school materials, or could we make do with the ones we bought last year? How would we pay for the new roof the church needed? Would our diocesan delegates be willing to pay their own expenses? Older parishioners spoke longingly of times when the church had been full and growing. A newcomer at Christ Church during my time was a rarity who was immediately spotted and surrounded by well-wishers. Confirmation classes numbered ten at most, often fewer. The parish membership remained stable while I was there, which I regarded as a victory. It was hard at times, but the people of the church and town embraced us and our young children with open arms. We loved living in Fairmont because we loved the people there. We still do.

Years later, as rector of St. Paul's, Daphne, I found a situation I could not have imagined during my time in Fairmont. Daphne was one of the fastest-growing areas in the South. Moving vans were in town every day — not to take furniture away, but to deliver it. New housing developments sprouted up on what had been farmland a year before. Stores, schools, hospitals, and churches were being built and staging "grand openings." During my ten years as rector of St. Paul's, both Sunday attendance and giving rose between three- and fourfold. We had trouble keeping track of all the newcomers, and confirmation classes of forty or more were common. When we began to overflow the old church, we built a new and larger one.

There were reasons for the growth other than the fact that I was happy at St. Paul's (I'd been happy at Christ Church, Fairmont, too). A lot of it had to do with location. Although the parish was situated on a back street, it was in a census tract that increased in population by 30 percent during the decade. Moreover, for part of the time, another Episcopal congregation down the road was in conflict, and some of its members sought a church elsewhere. Parishioners knew how to welcome newcomers, and new people were attracted by the warm, accepting atmosphere of St. Paul's. Because the parish managed to get good press coverage, a few new members came in because they had read about St. Paul's. It was exhilarating, tiring, satisfying, frightening, confusing, and fun. Sometimes it was all those things at once. I loved living in Daphne and serving at St. Paul's. Pam and I still love the people there, too.

Christ Church and St. Paul's were similar parishes in some ways. Both treated my family and me well, which made for happy leadership, and happy leadership made for a happy parish; it flowed both ways. Both numbered among their members more than the usual allotment of committed, hard-working Christians, the kind who gladden the heart of a pastor. Both tolerated dissent on controversial matters; neither was inclined to bicker. In both places, people laughed freely and didn't take themselves too seriously. I count myself twice blessed for having served at those two parishes.

These two experiences have taught me some things.

It's easier to get excited when the numbers are up than when the numbers are down. There's energy in both situations, but the feeling is different when you're building something than when you're struggling to hold on to something. In Fairmont, one curmudgeonly old vestryman said, when the bare-bones budget for the next year was announced, "I just want this church to stay open long enough for me to be buried from it!" At Daphne, I recall one vestryman saying, "Let's dream our wildest dream and then figure out how to make it come true!" There was energy in both remarks, but the feel could hardly have been more different.

Numbers never tell the whole story. It's easy to read too much into numbers. Small, dwindling churches aren't necessarily failures, nor are growing churches necessarily successes. Faithfulness, not size, should be the measure of success or failure in the church — and of course, faithfulness can't be measured. There are ways to grow a church that are not faithful, and there are times when living faithfully does not produce growth. I regard both Christ Church, Fairmont, and St. Paul's, Daphne, as successful parishes, because both carried out intentional and faithful ministries. If we were to think in terms of credit for good deeds (which of course we don't, since Christ has made the notion of credit superfluous), I suspect living faithfully in a struggling, marginal congregation would gain more points than living faithfully in a big, growing congregation.

Happiness has more to do with what's going on inside you than with what's going on outside. Both at Christ Church and at St. Paul's, there

were people who radiated joy. They saw God wherever they looked
and saw themselves as part of God's world. Therefore, they never complained. Merely to be in their presence was a cause for thanksgiving.
Both parishes also had a few suspicious people who saw trouble everywhere. The difference had to do not with what they saw but with the
meaning they gave to what they saw. I have learned the truth of this
in my own life as well. When I have been unhappy, I often blamed
outward circumstances and other people, even though the primary
cause of my unhappiness lay within me. Nothing outside myself can
make me either happy or unhappy. I was happy both in Fairmont and
in Daphne, although the outward circumstances were very different.
In both places, my happiness came from within.

God really is in charge. I worked equally hard in both parishes, and so
did the parishioners. I'm sure our hard work amounted to something,
but I suspect it amounted to less than we thought. Congregations, and
perhaps entire denominations, rise and fall. The reasons are many, and
most of the reasons have little to do with how hard people work or
don't work. I suspect it is more a matter of whether we are willing to
step out of the way and let God be God. Regardless of what we do, in
happy times and in distressing times, God will do what God will do.
Count on it. And God is good, which means that whatever is going on
or not going on in our parish, whether the numbers are up or down,
there is every reason to be radiant.

$\mathcal{N}$ _____ Nursing Homes

Elderly people are often overlooked in our youth-obsessed society, and those confined to their homes or to institutions are sometimes written off and forgotten. I regarded visiting them as one of the most sacred parts of my ministry. I or another priest on my staff tried to see each homebound or institution-bound parishioner once a month. Laypersons often visited as well. I usually had communion in the room and then remained for a time of conversation. These visits took a good bit of time, but they were often delightful, because elderly people have an abundance of stories to tell. Conversation was more difficult, though, with those whose minds were unclear. In such cases, I grew accustomed to hearing the same stories over and over again. *Telling such stories gave pleasure to these people,* I reminded myself, and every time I sat and listened, I thought of it as giving a gift. For those unable to speak at all, I struggled with what to do and say. I commented on the weather outside, current news, church events, or anything else I could think of, then prayed with the person and departed, wondering whether my brief visit had made any difference. Those were the hardest visits for me.

I also visited nursing homes occasionally to lead what was inaccurately called a "Bible study." No one brought a Bible, and if they had, most could not have read it. The "Bible study" consisted of a few remarks by me, combining reflections on the scriptures with personal anecdotes, and a few songs accompanied on the piano. The residents liked the singing better than my talking, so we spent most of the time singing. In every institution I ever visited, there was a strong preference for nineteenth-century gospel songs that the residents could sing from memory. Sometimes there was more swaying to the beat than singing, but I knew they knew what we were doing and that the songs stirred their souls. The Episcopal hymnal was of little use for that sort of music, so when I was playing the piano I took a Baptist hymnal with me.

Nurses' aides brought residents to these events in their wheelchairs. I could tell a lot about the institution by trying to engage the residents in conversation. In some places, they had a sparkle in their eyes and responded with humor to what I said, but in others, they looked dazed and hardly responded at all because sedatives were pumped into them around the clock. Some of the more expensive places were the worst offenders.

One of my happiest memories is of a conversation in a nursing home in Fairhope, Alabama. Sometimes I'm all primed for a word from the Lord, as when I'm meditating on a Bible passage or reading a book by a spiritual author, but nothing comes to me. I may as well be reading used car ads or the Sears catalog. But sometimes when I'm not even thinking about God, let alone expecting an inspirational rendezvous, God catches me up short by addressing me through the voice of someone I'd never have fancied a divine spokesperson. That's what happened in the nursing home that morning. I wasn't expecting a word from the Lord, and certainly not one spoken through a wheelchair-bound nursing home resident.

I was sitting in the social room thumbing through the hymnal while residents were being wheeled in. One of the residents said, to no one in particular, "I had the most *beautiful* cup of coffee this morning, and my cereal was *perfect!*" It was as if God had poked me in the ribs. I sat straight up in my chair and looked at the man. I had seen him many times before on these occasions, and I knew him. His name was Richard, and he was a parishioner of St. James' Church, a neighboring Episcopal congregation. Richard had been in a wheelchair for at least eight years, as long as I had been visiting that facility. If I had thought much about Richard (which I hadn't), I'd have guessed his wasn't a very happy life, confined as he was within the walls of that institution and to that wheelchair. But Richard practically bubbled with gratitude — *for a cup of coffee and a bowl of cereal!*

I too enjoy coffee and cereal in the morning, but I don't give them much thought. As I sip my coffee and eat my cereal, I'm more likely to be agitated about something. Like what I'm reading in the paper. Or my schedule of appointments for the day. Or my unanswered mail and unreturned phone messages. Or my feelings of guilt because I haven't found the time to do something. Or the person who spoke harshly to me yesterday and how unreasonable I think he or she was. Or the lack of money to accomplish some pet project. *Beautiful* coffee? *Perfect* cereal? I had never thought of them that way. Too many other things competed for space in my mind.

God spoke to me a second time a few moments later, again through Richard. After he had commented on his beautiful cup of coffee and his perfect cereal, I noticed he was wearing four or five strands of Mardi Gras beads. Readers unfamiliar with the Gulf Coast must understand that in that part of the country, life stops for two weeks in February or March of every year for a series of back-to-back parties and parades. Mardi Gras originated in Mobile, Alabama, before New Orleans took it up, and south Alabamians of every race and class still turn out for it. One of the things associated with Mardi Gras is plastic beads, the very definition of tackiness, but an essential part of Mardi Gras attire. I came to love wearing them. Richard was decked out in plastic beads, but this was November. I'd never seen anyone wear Mardi Gras beads in November. "Are those Mardi Gras beads?" I asked. He said they were. "But this is November," I said.

"Every day is Mardi Gras!" Richard exclaimed. Then he said something that just about leveled me: "Today is Mardi Gras because you have come! I always love it when you or one of the St. James' clergy comes to see us. You look so good in your Episcopal collar! You're the reason today is Mardi Gras!"

Why is it that I, with so much to be thankful for, so rarely pause to give thanks, while Richard, with so much less, gives thanks for a mere cup of coffee? And why is it that I, who can dance and frolic whenever I wish, so rarely do so, while Richard, confined to his wheelchair, celebrates Mardi Gras every day?

Ordination

In 1970, one other young man was ordained to the priesthood at the same time I was. The ordination took place at St. Matthew's Church in Charleston, West Virginia, where the other ordinand was curate. One of the things I remember about my ordination was that his relatives and well-wishers gave him lots of gifts. I received few gifts, because almost no one I knew attended my ordination, and if they had, they wouldn't have known it was an occasion for giving gifts. Not one person from St. Stephen's, Romney, the congregation I had served for the previous six months, attended. It was a six-hour drive from Romney to Charleston, along two-lane mountain roads. None of this bothered me; I did not feel slighted or unappreciated. I saw the event in largely utilitarian terms: it authorized me to do what I wanted to do with my life.

Other priests, however, feel differently about their ordinations. Many commemorate the anniversary of their ordination with a retreat or special celebration of the Holy Eucharist. I never felt a need to do that. In fact, I don't remember the date of my ordination. Many clergy also frame their ordination certificates and hang them on their office walls. I didn't do that, either, since I prefer watercolors, woodcuts, sconces, and the like on my walls. Some clergy also add a small cross (or plus sign) after their signatures, signifying that they are priests, which I've never done.

When I've asked my colleagues why they celebrate their ordination anniversaries, frame their ordination certificates, and add the sign of the cross to their signatures, they tell me it's because their priesthood is important to them. Some even say that priesthood is a fundamental part of who they are and that without it they would feel like a different person. When they tell me this, I give them what I fear is a blank, uncomprehending stare. I loved my life as a parish priest for thirty years and still enjoy the continuing opportunities I have to exercise my priestly ministry in retirement. I would do it over again, but I never felt ordination defined who I was. Maybe I have a "low" theology of priesthood. As a matter of fact, someone once told me I don't have *any* theology of the priesthood.

In the Catholic tradition, of which the Episcopal Church is a part, priests can do three things which laypersons don't do. They are as easy to remember as ABC — absolution (the formal declaration that God forgives sin), blessing (the dedication of objects for sacred use and the authoritative declaration of God's care and favor), and consecrating (of the bread and wine of communion). I'm glad somebody does those things, but I never cared who did them and would have been just as happy had it been someone else. I sought ordination because I wanted to preach and teach and work in the church, and it's easier to get a job doing that if you're ordained. The ABC part was included in the package, so I did those things, too.

One day it occurred to me that the reason I had never paid much attention to my ordination was that I didn't feel even slightly different from other people on account of it. I knew I was a sinner, and my ordination didn't change that. I also knew that God loved and accepted me, but that was true long before I was ordained. Ordination simply defined my ministry. Others had ministries in the church, too: they sang in the choir, swept the floors, balanced the books, taught the children. My particular ministry required an advanced degree and that the bishop lay his hands on my head, and it paid a salary. But underneath all that, it was just one of many Christian ministries. I saw myself as part of the body essentially, as a leader of the body incidentally.

Then I had another idea about those little crosses that clergy place after their names. Why don't all Christians sign their names that way? The sign of the cross is customarily made upon a person's forehead when she is baptized, not when she is ordained. I wrote an article for a clergy journal once suggesting we invite the laity to join us in adding plus signs to our signatures so that whenever a Christian signs his name, he will be reminded of his baptism. Nothing came of my suggestion.

As I mulled over all this, my baptism became increasingly important to me, for baptism is what makes someone part of the communion of saints. What about my own baptism? I wanted to know when God had publicly announced his love for me, that Richard Hanna Schmidt was one of his own. I knew I had been baptized as a young child, both because my parents assured me of it and because I dimly remembered the occasion. My younger brother and I were baptized on the same day, and I recall misbehaving during the ceremony. But how old was I? When did that event occur? My parents retained no record of my baptism. I wrote to the pastor of the First Presbyterian Church of Shelbyville, Kentucky, where the baptism had taken place. He wrote back that the records of the church from the 1940s were in disarray in the bottom of a flooded bank vault and that it might be impossible to learn the date of my baptism. I was disappointed to receive his letter, but I had lived happily for forty years without knowing the date, so I figured I could continue to do so. I put it out of my mind.

But the pastor did not forget my inquiry. Three years later, I received another letter from him: "I was in the bank vault this week sorting through the damaged church records, and I came across the record of your baptism. You were baptized on April 4, 1948." I remember trembling as I gazed at the paper on which the date was written. I looked it up immediately. April 4 was the Sunday after Easter that year. That is the Sunday when we read about Thomas, the outsider, who was not with the others when Jesus appeared to them that first Easter night and who couldn't bring himself to believe the implausible tale they told him when he returned. *How very fitting,* I thought. I'd always identified with Thomas. I was delighted to have been baptized on the day the church recalls the event for which Thomas is chiefly remembered. The Second Sunday of Easter has now become my own personal holy day. Each year, I say special prayers that day to thank God for receiving me into his loving arms. That's the anniversary that's important to me.

Prayer I

"I will pray for you." I must have said those words more than a thousand times. I said them to dying cancer patients and their loved ones, husbands and wives in troubled marriages, alcoholics flirting with recovery, would-be believers who had lost their faith, penitents burdened with guilt, grieving widows, people out of work, victims of abuse, adults troubled by childhood memories, and my own children as they left home for college. Often I promised to pray for someone in response to a request that I do so; sometimes I made the promise as much for myself as for the person prayed for.

But what does it mean to say, "I will pray for you"? I usually meant that I intended to add the person's name to the parish's prayer list, which was printed in the weekly newsletter and read aloud every Sunday in church. But I also meant that I personally would pray for the person.

Sometimes I didn't do as I had promised. When Pam and I had young children in the house, private prayer was a struggle for me. I had little or no quiet time in those days. My praying was sometimes little more than a good intention, and I felt guilty when I didn't do it. What sort of a quack was I, standing in the pulpit week after week, when I didn't even say my prayers?

That changed as I grew older. In middle age, and especially now that I am retired, I more easily find quiet time at home. Taking an hour or so for prayer and devotion each day is now a luxury I enjoy as much as anything I do. I call it a luxury because I realize today what I didn't know earlier — intentional, focused, daily prayer is a gift granted only to some people and only at certain times. I once thought there was something called "the faithful life" which didn't change, but was a constant, to be aimed at until achieved. Daily prayer was a nonnegotiable part of it. Now, though, I see that life has its stages, or "chapters," as Martin Marty calls them. The Preacher of Ecclesiastes might have said (but didn't quite say) that there is a time to pray and a time a time to refrain from praying. You do what you can do when you can do it, give thanks that you can do it, then don't feel guilty about what you can't do.

Now that God has given me the luxury of leisurely prayer, I rise daily at around 6:00 a.m., wash and dress quickly, and then sit down with a cup of coffee. There's nothing sacred about the early morning hour; it's just the time that suits me. I begin with a few moments of quiet. In seasonable weather, I sit outside where I can welcome the rising sun to the new day and hear the birds, crickets, wind, and early-morning traffic. I thank God for these sights and sounds and for his creatures who produce them. I thank him for another day begun in good health. I thank him for my breath, my firm chair, the shirt on my back, those I love, who are still asleep in their beds. I thank God for the capacity to express my thanks. Then I read a few passages from scripture, pausing to reflect on sentences and phrases that catch my imagination and placing myself in the scene when the passage lends itself to that. I usually read a chapter from a devotional book and then meditate on a hymn text or a poem. Among poets, I often return to John Donne, George Herbert, Gerard Manley Hopkins, Emily Dickinson, and T. S. Eliot. I then review the day ahead of me, visualizing the people I expect to see, the tasks I will face, and the decisions I must make, entrusting each moment of the day to God's guidance and grace.

Then I am ready to pray for others. I begin with the Anglican and diocesan prayer cycles, then the parish prayer list, and then my personal prayer list. I once kept my own prayer list on a single sheet of paper, but my eye tended to drift hurriedly over the names and I sometimes skipped a few names. Then, about ten years ago, I began writing each name on a blank calling card. Now I look at one name at a time, pausing to call to mind the face of the person, then envisioning the grace and power of God, in the form of a gentle light, surrounding the face. Such a prayer list is easily updated by removing or adding a card. I never throw a card away, which enables me occasionally to return to the past and pray once more for those who requested my prayers months or years ago. In some cases I have lost track of these people, but I can still visualize their faces and pray for them when I reach back into the archives of my prayer cards.

That concludes my daily prayer time. Then comes a bowl of cereal and the morning paper. Having prayed before turning to the newspaper makes for greater serenity when reading the news. Sometimes something in the paper moves me to pray again.

Does this praying do any good? I believe it helps others, but I'm never sure. I know it helps me. It reminds me that I, together with those I pray for, depend on God, and that all of us depend on one another. My favorite quotation about private prayer comes from Richard Hooker: "When we are not able to do any other thing for men's behoof, when through maliciousness or unkindness they vouchsafe not to accept any other good at our hands, prayer is that which we always have in our power to bestow, and they never in theirs to refuse."

Prayer II

My daily hour of prayer and meditation is usually a happy, contented time for me. When I can envision the coming day as flowing smoothly (which is of course no guarantee that it *will* flow smoothly), my prayers usually flow smoothly as well. But when I face a perplexing decision or a tense situation, my prayers often jam up. I cannot see beyond my problem, and I stew in it. Sometimes I awaken at three in the morning, muscles tense and stressed. I try to pray, but my prayers seem hollow, wooden, nothing but words. I can't focus on God, much less on trusting God and surrendering my will to God.

What to do? I have discovered several ways to get my prayers unstuck. None is foolproof and none works every time, but each has helped. Here are some things to do when you can't pray:

Write. Writing down your thoughts and feelings can help clarify them. Sometimes I don't even know what is bothering me until I begin to write. What comes out onto the paper is occasionally suitable for sharing, but more often it is private in nature. Writing is itself a kind of prayer for me; God and I speak to one another through the written page, and what emerges in those conversations sometimes startles me.

Visualize yourself and the other people involved in your dilemma surrounded by a warm, clear light. If you have a problem with a particular person, take a few extra moments to visualize the light surrounding that person. If you must make a decision, let the light envelop all the people and places affected by the decision. Allow the radiant scene to linger in your mind.

Read the Psalms. The best way is to read just one psalm or a few verses of a longer psalm slowly and repeatedly. Let the words seep through your soul. You will probably find a soul mate in one or more of the psalmists. Let the psalm become a prayer for you. Hymn texts and written prayers from various sources can help in the same way.

Seek out a trusted confidant. This is especially important if your immobilization in prayer continues for an extended time. This can be done either in person or over the telephone. Although that person won't give you a simple, step-by-step way out of your difficulty (because there is no such way), your mind will usually be calmed simply by sharing your dilemma with someone else. I always ask my confidant to pray with and for me, which means the prayers of someone whose soul is not obstructed are added to my own. It is as if my friend's prayers, flowing freely around my dilemma, somehow gather up my own paralyzed prayers and carry them along. In time, the logjam within me is broken down.

Remind yourself who is in charge. Regardless of what we do or decide, all will be well in the end, because God will still be God. This perplexity, like all perplexities before it, will pass, and clarity will someday be restored to us. God will continue to love us, and even if we do the wrong thing, God will still be there, arms open wide, to forgive and heal us when we see our error and return to him. I sometimes get the notion that God is even chuckling as I stew in my dilemma, saying something to himself like, *Just look at that silly Richard down there, wallowing and stumbling around in his mud. Won't he be surprised when he finally realizes that what he does or doesn't do isn't all that important, that the only thing that matters is that I love him!*

$\mathcal{Q}$ _____ Questions

Death is a not a tragedy. It is a good and natural thing, and the Bible often refers to it in benign terms such as being "gathered to our fathers." On one memorable day in 1999 I buried two parishioners, aged ninety-three and ninety-one. Both funerals were occasions for celebration rather than for sadness. Each woman had been a pioneer of a sort, exercising leadership in the church at a time when few women were admitted to leadership positions. Each had enjoyed a full and fruitful life and grown frail in her old age. Neither was afraid to die. Both had been ready, even eager, for their "entrance into the land of light and joy." Testimonies of loving friends and well-wishers marked their departures from this life. These were holy deaths, and if there were tears, they were tears of thanksgiving.

Death is part of God's plan. The fact that we die keeps life from becoming an empty exercise of meaningless motion. If there were no death, we could bring no children into the world. The same fixed number of souls would live from eon to eon, neither growing nor dying nor giving birth, never older, never wiser. There would be nothing to accomplish or discover or conquer or experience for the first time, no mountains to climb, no risks to take, no choices to make, no fear of hell, no hope of heaven. We would soon cease to possess functioning souls and become listless, mindless bodies drifting endlessly about. Life would be rooted in no reality beyond what could be seen outside any window.

Our problem with death is not with death itself, but with certain deaths. On October 31, 1973, ordained just three years, I was beginning my third week as priest in charge of St. John's, Charleston, after the departure of the two senior priests who had supervised me until the month before. That morning the phone rang. It was the church office calling to inform me that the daughter of a vestryman had been murdered the night before in a San Francisco parking lot by the Black Panther terrorist group, apparently a random slaying. The next several days were a blur for me, and probably for the family. I went with them to the funeral home to identify the sliced-up body of their daughter and sister. I discussed the funeral with them and then conducted the service. I spent hours in their home. Perhaps never in my life have I felt so inadequate. This was only my second funeral. What was I supposed to do? What could I say to these people? How could I assuage their loss? Comforting words did not come to me. I tried to think of something, anything to say, but everything that came to mind seemed like a cliché unworthy of the moment. Despite my theological education, I couldn't think coherently about such an event, much less speak coherently of it. I was embarrassed at my inability to say anything significant. So when I said anything, it was a passing comment on some idle topic like the weather or the food friends had brought to the house. Most of the time I sat with the family, teary eyed, saying nothing.

It is all very well to say that death is part of God's plan, but why does God allow someone's daughter to die at such a young age? Why with such pain and suffering? As a result of senseless violence? When she could still have contributed so much? When others loved and needed her? The deaths of children and teenagers were always the most difficult for me, and most difficult of all were teen suicides. I dealt with three teen suicides during my years as a parish priest. What possible sense could there be to such a tragedy? What is there to say?

I shall never forget what the mother of the young woman murdered by the Black Panthers said to me after her daughter's funeral: "You will never know how much your words meant to us." This expression of gratitude astonished me because I knew I had said nothing of any substance. What words could she possibly have meant? When I mentioned this later to an older, more experienced priest, he said the mother's remark didn't surprise him. "It doesn't matter what you say," he explained. "It's that you were there. Your presence and your tears were the best gift you could have given them. That's what they heard."

The right words are not necessary or maybe even possible in times of tragedy, but the wrong words can be devastating. People often try to make mourners stop grieving. But to grieve is natural, even essential, if healing is to come, and grief often includes anger, confusion, despondency, and doubt. This is true even for those with deep religious faith, and words that invalidate grief are not of God. One of the most honest and helpful books on this topic that I know of is C. S. Lewis's *A Grief Observed,* in which the great Christian teacher asks all the hard questions following the death of his wife and dismisses all the easy answers. Lewis does not flinch in the darkness. "It's God's will," someone often says. That's hogwash. It is only God's will in that God allows a world in which tragedy can occur, but if God picks and chooses certain souls upon whom to inflict searing pain, then we should resist God, not serve him. "God has taken her to be with him in heaven," someone else will say. More hogwash. A God who would choose to take someone away in the prime of life from those who love her because he wants her with him in heaven is a vicious God, and I refuse to serve him. "This is part of God's grand plan, which we cannot know," someone else will say. Not quite hogwash. I believe God does have a grand plan and that God is able to take a human tragedy and work it into his plan (the crucifixion of Jesus is the best example of that), but God's plan doesn't include his arbitrarily torturing selected persons. What do these people mean when they speak of God's grand plan? Do they envision their God sitting on his heavenly throne and saying, "Sam, you get fired today. Henry, you win the lottery. A healthy baby for Alice, a sick baby for Hazel. Sandra, a hurricane blows your house away today, and for you, Bob, a fatal car crash"? No, if that's the kind of God you believe in, keep him to yourself; I want no part of him.

I eventually found some things to say in the face of tragedy, but they address tragedy only on the intellectual level and they don't make us feel better when the pain is specific and our own. It's easy to theorize why God might allow pain and tragedy. A world with no pain would be no better than a world with no death. A car traveling at high speed toward a ditch would stop whether or not the driver applied the brake; a killer's bullet would turn to jelly before striking its victim; a mountain climber losing his grip would drift harmlessly to the ground; a deadly virus would be rendered inert just as it enters your lungs. There would be no sciences because science requires enduring structures to investigate. Such a world would have no laws of nature because nature would be forever adjusting her ways so as to inflict no pain. In the absence of pain, there would be no need for generosity, forgiveness, kindness, sacrifice, loyalty, commitment, work, or love. That would be a very different world from the world God created. I suppose God placed us in this world because human beings are not "finished" creatures, but rough models that require growth and refining, and God knew the kind of environment in which the growth and refining we need could take place. So there is tragedy in the world, and there is injustice, want, sorrow, death — boundless opportunities for generosity, forgiveness, kindness, and the like. This is an intellectual answer to the problem of pain. Some people find it satisfactory, as an intellectual exercise, but it doesn't help when your daughter is murdered.

Even this explanation does not fully address the problem of pain. What about pain intentionally inflicted by one person on another? Earthquakes and tornadoes are one thing, but why does God allow war, genocide, murders of innocent young women in parking lots, and the countless little acts of cruelty we inflict on one another every day? These evils are the consequences of decisions resulting from human freedom. Freedom is a gift, not a curse. God creates us for the purpose of entering into a relationship of love, obedience, and joy with him. He could have programmed us so that we would invariably adore him and follow his instructions, like robots or computers, but then we would not be free. For love, obedience, and joy to have meaning, they must be freely chosen, and that means the choice of hatred, disobedience, and misery must also be open to us. Freedom is risky, but it's a risk God takes every time a baby is born. God will not stop us, however destructively we may behave. He is willing to endure the consequences of our freedom in order to hold open the possibility of our love. I doubt this is any easier for God than it is for us. God honors us by saying to us, "*Thy* will be done; have it *your* way." Human freedom is God's will, of course — but not every act that results from it is God's will. This also is a merely intellectual answer, though, and it isn't worth a nickel when your daughter is murdered.

It has often been pointed out that in Christian thinking, not only does God not inflict pain and suffering on his people, but — and this is, so far as I know, a uniquely Christian understanding — God identifies with the suffering. This identifying is no mere sympathy from a distance, but an entering into the midst of human suffering and enduring the horror of it himself. Only Christians worship a bleeding, crucified God; the very idea of such a God is inconceivable or blasphemous to other faiths. What this means for Christians is that however grievous our life may be, God has walked this way before us. Pain, tragedy, death, and all the rest of it can be encounters with the divine. They can also, of course, induce despair and nihilism. It has to do, I think, with what you're looking for. Those who lack eyes to see God will not see him, even in a resplendent sunset, whereas those with eyes to see God will see him everywhere, even in the darkest dungeon.

Fourteenth-century Europe was a bleak time. The Black Death was devastating the continent, wiping out as much as half the population in many areas, while the brutal and pointless Hundred Years' War dragged on between France and England. Most of the literature, theology, and art of the day contains dire warnings and visions of the torments of hell. It is remarkable that such a time could produce someone like Julian of Norwich. Julian spent fifty years in a small cell attached to a church in Norwich, England, giving counsel to those who sought her out and writing a book of reflections on a series of sixteen visions of God she had received on the afternoon of May 13, 1373. The book's recurring theme is the goodness of God. Julian saw God's beauty, generosity, grace, and courtesy in every moment, every event, and every person. She wrote, " . . . there are many deeds which in our eyes are so evilly done and lead to such great harms that it seems to us impossible that any good result could ever come of them. . . . And the cause is this: that the reason which we use is now so blind, so abject and so stupid that we cannot recognize God's exalted, wonderful wisdom, or the power and the goodness of the blessed Trinity." In perhaps the best-known passage from her book, Julian wrote, "And so our good Lord answered all the questions and doubts which I could raise, saying most comfortingly: I may make all things well, and I can make all things well, and I shall make all things well . . . and you will see yourself that every kind of thing will be well."

Nearly four hundred years later, Jean-Pierre de Caussade, a French Jesuit, wrote a series of letters to a group of nuns for whom he served as spiritual director. These were later collected into a volume called *Abandonment to Divine Providence,* which has helped many who sought a glimpse of God under tragic circumstances. He wrote:

> No matter what troubles, unhappiness, worries, upsets, doubts and needs harass souls who have lost all confidence in their own powers, they can all be overcome by the marvelous hidden and unknown power of the divine action. The more perplexing the situation, the more we can hope for a happy solution. The heart says, "All will be well. God has the matter in hand. We need fear nothing." Our very fear and sense of desolation are verses in this hymn of darkness. We delight in singing every syllable of them, knowing that all ends with the "Glory be to the Father."

In God's time, in God's way, God will sort out all things and make all things well. It is God, not we, who will do this; if the job of sorting things out and making things well were ours, we would botch it up. When my loved ones die — and when the time comes for me to die, if I am given time to consider my death and if I have my wits about me — I hope I shall rest securely in God's arms, allowing him to carry me to that place where sorrow and pain are no more. Then finally, when I've arrived and he's seen me settled in, I hope God will grant me a few minutes one-on-one — because I have some questions.

Recovery

As I write these words, I have been a recovering alcoholic for twenty-one years, and while my addiction has been public knowledge for most of that time, I don't often speak of it. As with many alcoholics, my disease developed over a period of years. As a young man, I found alcohol relieved the stress that arose from what I now perceive as my compulsive perfectionism. I had determined early on to be the best Christian, priest, husband, father, and friend anyone had ever known — and I had hoped to be recognized as such. That this feat was beyond human capacity I might have granted in theory, but I aimed for it all the same. When things didn't work out perfectly and I began to see that life's decisions were more complex and ambiguous than I had thought, I became tense and disillusioned. A shot of bourbon (I am a Kentuckian, and there would be no question as to my booze of choice) helped soothe the tension. Then it took two shots. Then I stopped measuring.

Only my wife, Pam, was aware of my growing addiction at first, but by 1983, in my first year as rector of St. Peter's, Ladue, I had come to realize that my life was reeling out of control. Repeated attempts to moderate my drinking had been unsuccessful. I had the sense that I was tottering on the brink of a precipice, peering down at sharp rocks hundreds of feet below. If I didn't do something, I would fall headlong upon the rocks and perish. I was terrified. I consulted with a friend and fellow priest who was in recovery. He suggested I visit ninety meetings of Alcoholics Anonymous in ninety days — one meeting a day for three months. "But I've got responsibilities," I said. "I don't have that kind of time!" My friend asked whether I could name anything more important than getting my alcoholism under control. "No," I said, "because if I don't do that, I'm going to lose everything else, my job, my family, my health, my life, everything. I'll find a way to do it." And I did.

Like most newly recovering alcoholics, I was keen that my addiction remain a secret. I found it embarrassing. If the knowledge got out, I thought it might adversely affect my career. I dreaded the day someone would recognize me at an A.A. meeting. That happened at my third meeting. I had not spoken, but a St. Peter's parishioner had seen me across the room and approached me afterward. "Dick, I think it's great that you've come to this open meeting to learn about this disease so that you can help your parishioners," she said.

"Well — I may as well tell you the real reason I'm here," I said hesitantly. She broke into a big smile. In the days and weeks that followed, I saw her and several other parishioners at meetings. I hadn't known that anyone from St. Peter's was a recovering alcoholic, but I found myself surrounded by new friends, some of whom were parishioners I had known before, but not really known. And I needn't have worried about anonymity, for no recovering person has ever violated my anonymity.

Not surprisingly, I began to notice the extent of other people's drinking for the first time. Alcohol was an accepted part of parish life at St. Peter's. Liquor was served at some parish social functions, and while most parishioners drank responsibly, some did not. Drunkenness, when it occurred, was tolerated and not acknowledged. We all pretended it wasn't happening. I began to see this as something other than normal, healthy behavior, but I said nothing, reluctant to reveal my alcoholism and recovery to the parish.

One day, after I had been in recovery just eighteen months, a woman in the parish came to see me about her troubled marriage. I quickly perceived that a major part of the problem was her husband's alcoholism and her codependence. Believing it might help her if she knew my own story, I told her of my addiction and recovery, asking her to keep the information confidential. Shortly thereafter, Stan Pylipow, my senior warden, pulled me aside after a vestry meeting. "Have you heard the rumors circulating in the parish?" he asked. No, I hadn't. "People are saying you have a bottle of liquor in your desk drawer and are drunk by noon every day. They say you beat your wife when you're drunk and that she's about to divorce you." The woman had not merely betrayed my confidence, but magnified and distorted what I had confided to her.

Stan was a wise and loyal counselor to me and one of the most exemplary Christians I had ever known. When I told him the truth, which was of course far less damaging than the rumors, he and I agreed that the only way to deal with the rumors was to tell the truth publicly. In November 1984, I preached my "I am an alcoholic" sermon, based on John Newton's famous hymn "Amazing Grace." The grace of God had saved a wretch like me, I said. Grace had taught my heart to fear, and grace my fears relieved.

I wept profusely in the pulpit that day, not knowing what the fallout from that sermon would be. I need not have been concerned. Some parishioners who had been chummy with me before became more distant — because of unwillingness to look at their own drinking? — but others who had been courteous but not close now warmed to me. In retrospect, I believe that sermon broke through a veil of denial at St. Peter's. For the first time, alcoholism was on the table and could be discussed openly. Not everyone wanted or needed to discuss it, but it was no longer a secret. And perhaps best of all, three days after the sermon, a friend in the parish whose drinking I had known nothing about came into my office. "If you can stand up in the pulpit and say that about yourself, I guess I can sit in your office and tell you about myself," he said. He entered alcoholism recovery that day, and two other St. Peter's parishioners entered recovery in the weeks that followed.

Eventually I was able to trace the rumors to the woman with the alcoholic husband. She continued to come to church, but would not look me in the eye after that sermon and never acknowledged to me that she had started the rumors. Years later, when I was preparing to leave the parish, I wanted to bid her farewell, although I did not intend to mention alcohol or the rumors. Three times I phoned and made an appointment to see her, and three times she canceled the appointment. I was never able to tell her good-bye, but I continued to pray for her.

Now, more than twenty years since I entered alcoholism recovery, I credit that program with the fact that I am a healthy and contented person today. My preaching, counseling, and personal relationships have changed as a result of it. I now see all of life through that lens, almost as if recovery principles have become part of my very breathing. And most of all, alcoholism recovery has brought me closer to God than any other influence in my life, with the exception of my family of origin. And to think that I hadn't even known I was ill.

 **Religion**

I ran across the following item a few years ago in "Notes and Queries," a sometimes dubious but always entertaining column in my favorite British newspaper, *The Guardian:*

> Q. What is the world's only true religion and how do we know?
>
> A. There is no true religion at present. I shall not be starting it until May. You will know because I shall tell you so.
>
> — Graham Gifford, Balcolyn, NSW, Australia

I don't know who Graham Gifford is. Perhaps there is no such person, but if there is, I think I'd like him. His comment reminded me of a more serious reflection written fifty years earlier by the man I regard as the twentieth century's greatest theologian, Karl Barth. The following little gem is buried in the deep recesses of Barth's ponderous *Church Dogmatics* (Volume II, VI, 31, i): "Every genuine proclamation of the Christian faith is a force disturbing to, even destructive of, the advance of religion. . . . It is bound to be so. Olympus and Valhalla decrease in population when the message of the God who is the one and only God is really known and believed. The figures of every religious culture are necessarily secularized and recede. They can keep themselves alive only as ideas, symbols, and ghosts, and finally as comic figures. And in the end even in this form they sink into oblivion."

It wasn't merely non-Christian religions that Barth had in mind. He was also speaking of his own religion, my own religion. Barth distrusted all religions because he felt they invariably fall short of

God, and religious people tend to turn them into idols, worshiping religion rather than God.

I agree with Barth — and with Graham Gifford, if I got his drift. No religion is or could ever be true. Only God is true. Those who insist on a certain liturgy, musical style, biblical interpretation, or form of church government are putting their religion where God should be. Religion can point us toward God, but to do so, it must point away from itself — that is to say, it must be willing to die. Barth says that when God is really known, religious figures are reduced to ideas, symbols, ghosts, and comic figures. That's true, but it's also true that God can come to us through such things. Comic figures are perhaps most useful of all because, unlike ideas, symbols, and ghosts, it is hard to take them too seriously. We are closest to God, I believe, when we laugh at our religions, ideas, and symbols — and at ourselves. It's hard to be pompous when you're laughing at yourself. Humor is humbling.

A serious religion is a dangerous religion. It contains too many periods and not enough question marks. In taking itself so seriously, such a religion invites its adherents to idolize it, eliminating God and erecting a statue of itself in God's place. Once our religion becomes an idol, knowing, worshiping, and serving God takes a back seat to convincing everyone that our religion is the true one.

As a boy, I took my religion very seriously. Everything seemed clear to me in those early days — right was right, wrong was wrong, and that was that. Lining up on the right side was serious business. That clarity of vision vanished when I began to grow up, but I still took religion seriously. It wasn't until I'd been ordained a few years that I saw the humor, even the silliness of most religious acts. I am an Episcopalian, but I know enough about other religious traditions to know that they are no less humorous than my own. As a professional Episcopalian, I dealt with cumbersome canons and regulations; attended liturgies that

were sometimes mundane, sometimes pompous; pretended to understand incomprehensible doctrines; sang unsingable songs; consumed
tasteless bread and cheap wine; dressed up in flamboyant outfits on
Sundays; and served on boring committees, commissions, and conventions that squabbled about things that didn't matter. But I love
my religion, for all its faults and foibles, including the institutional
casing in which it comes to me. Outsiders may wonder how I could
love such a thing. It's because God reaches out to me through my religion, challenges me, redeems me, and re-creates me. Had it not been
for the Christian church, I'd have never known that God loves me.
Given some of the things the church says and does, I believe that's a
miracle — and that's why I love my religion.

Retirement

For most of my working life I thought I'd retire at sixty-five, but a few years ago the Church Pension Fund made it possible for pastors to retire after thirty years on the job, regardless of their age. That was because studies showed that a number of clergy in their late fifties and early sixties were "hanging on" in parishes where they were no longer effective, while younger clergy were denied opportunities for advancement.

That sounded on target to me. Pam and I had seen other clergy, some of them our friends, who had remained in their parishes too long. They had enjoyed fruitful and happy ministries for several years, but the wind had gone out of their sails. Both parish and pastor would have benefited from a new challenge, but it didn't happen. Sometimes it was because the pastor couldn't find another position. Sometimes it was because he was comfortable and well paid and didn't want to move. Sometimes it was because his sense of who he was had become enmeshed with the parish, and he couldn't imagine himself anywhere else. And sometimes he had simply worked too hard and too long, often at low pay, and had burned out. Whatever the reason, these clergy finished their careers by simply putting in time. Parish and pastor began treading water, going nowhere, repeating the same tired programs year after year. Morale plummeted. Eventually, perceptive laypeople in the parish realized what was happening, but they were powerless to effect a change. Early in my career I had vowed this would not happen to me. When I realized it was time to go, I would go.

This possibility became more than a theoretical one for me when the Church Pension Fund began allowing clergy to retire after thirty years. Adding my pension payment to Pam's and my savings, Social Security, and some part-time work after retirement, we realized that a full-time salary was no longer necessary for us. At age fifty-five, we found ourselves with a choice. It's not that I didn't love parish work. I did and still do. Parish ministry had usually been good to me, and when it wasn't, I learned and grew from the experience, becoming a better person by learning to trust God. Moreover, the parish I had served for the last ten years was, I thought, the best parish in the Anglican Communion — relaxed, tolerant, generous, vital, and loving. Serving among such people had been a gift to me. I often asked myself what I had done to deserve such happiness. But after ten years, I knew I needed to go. A decade earlier, I had had a vision for the place, and seeing that vision realized had been a delight. Alleluia, hosanna, whoop-de-doo! — but now what? I had no vision for the next ten years. Clearly, it was time to go, both for my sake and for the parish's.

Pam's and my choice was whether to retire or move into another parish. I felt sure I could land another parish job if I wished, but having served in the best parish in the Anglican Communion, where else would I be happy? When Pam and I realized we could afford to retire, the decision was an easy one. Besides, there were lots of things we'd wanted to do in later life, and now, while our health was good, was the time to do them. I had noticed that those who wake up on the first day of their retirement and say, "Gee, what can I do today?" soon wither away. The retirees who flourish are those who plan in advance to do things they've always dreamt of doing. That's what Pam and I wanted.

During my first year of retirement, Pam and I traveled, bought a new home (in St. Louis, seven hundred miles from my last parish, so as not to complicate the arrival of my successor), and spent time on two seminary campuses where I wrote a book on Anglican theologians, now in its second printing. This book is my second, and a devotional book on the Psalms will be my third. I'm under contract for a fourth book, a new history of Christian spirituality. In 2002, I went to Nigeria for three months, ostensibly to teach at a theological school and lead conferences for diocesan clergy (which I did), but actually because I wanted to learn firsthand about life in a Third World country (which I also did). A year later, Pam and I spent three months in England, where I taught and we traveled. I now teach at a local seminary here in St. Louis, train overseas missionaries for the Episcopal Church, lead vestry retreats and clergy conferences, volunteer as an English teacher to Somali and Afghan refugees, and work two days a week at a local parish. And the list of things I want to do is still long.

Perhaps the most liberating feature of my retirement occurs at Grace Church, Kirkwood, Missouri, where I now serve as a part-time, sometime assistant priest. When someone approaches me on Sunday morning about a scheduling conflict, a typo in the bulletin, a budget shortfall, or something the General Convention has done, it is with secret glee (or maybe it's not so secret) that I say, "You need to talk to the rector about that!"

The joy I'm finding in retirement has confirmed for me yet again something I have learned repeatedly during my adult life but which I didn't know when I was younger: Everything changes, including people, including me. I could do some things when I was young that I can no longer do, and I can do some things now that I could not have done then. Moreover, what needed doing in the past is not what needs doing now. "New occasions teach new duties," as James Russell Lowell said. One of the keys to a happy life is to remain always open to fresh challenges, and to do that, we must let go of yesterday's challenges. The alternative is to live out our later years among listless memories, which would be to check out of life. I want never to do that.

# Sabbath

Waiting drives some people bonkers. They grow angry if required to stand in line for five minutes at the supermarket checkout. Idling at a traffic light for thirty seconds makes them squirm. If their spouse is not ready to leave the house when they are, they seethe and make sarcastic remarks. They like fast food when eating out and instant meals when eating in. They look at their watches habitually, compulsively, even when the time of day doesn't matter.

One day in 1979 I tripped on an uneven sidewalk and broke my wristwatch on the pavement. The watch was an antique and an heirloom, and I wanted it repaired, but when I took the watch to the jeweler, he told me the cost of repairing it would be nearly two hundred dollars, a huge sum to me in those days. I decided to wait a few weeks before authorizing the work. Soon I noticed an odd thing: I continued to look at my wrist, even when I didn't care about the time of day — and even though no watch was there. Checking my wrist had become a habit. A few days later a woman came to my office to seek consolation following the loss of her husband. Several times while she was speaking I looked at my wrist. When I realized what this must have said to the woman — "I'm busy, so hurry up and finish what you have to say" — I was mortified. How many times had I insulted people by looking at my watch while they were talking to me? I decided never to wear a watch again. If I needed to know the time, I would glance at the car dashboard, listen to the radio, pick up the telephone, look at a wall in a public building, or ask someone.

I quickly developed the ability to know the time intuitively, and not once in the more than two decades since I stopped wearing a watch have I been late for an appointment because I didn't know the time.

Not wearing a wristwatch also liberated me from a constraint I hadn't known had bound me. I grew less compulsive about time. In the early years of my career, I had felt guilty when I "wasted" time, did something not deemed useful. I took my day off once a week and rarely compromised it, but even on my day off, I felt I should be accomplishing something — cleaning the basement, pulling weeds, working out, building relationships, studying, shopping for what I needed or thought I needed. I planned my time around such tasks. My day off always had an agenda, and it didn't include taking a nap, sitting in the garden, reading a cheap novel, or simply playing — because those activities were *useless.*

Only after I stopped wearing a watch did I come to see how healing it can be to do nothing. The key to contentment is not to achieve something, even something for God, but to *know* God. To know someone, whether God or another person, requires spending time together — laughing, playing, cutting up, doing nothing, wasting time. It had been that way with Pam and me. Before we realized we wanted to spend our lives together, we had passed many hours simply enjoying one another's company, doing nothing in particular. If that hadn't come first, I doubt we'd have ever grown to love each other. We came to love each other because we often forgot about time when we were together.

When I was eleven years old, my parents took my brother, my sister, and me to Washington, D.C., for a week. Each day my mother tried to take us to a different museum, federal monument, or other culturally ennobling spot. My father held out for a trip to Griffith Stadium, where the old Washington Senators used to lose baseball games. My mother prevailed for several days until finally my father had enough and packed us all into the car for a trip to the ballpark. Today I don't remember any of the museums, but I remember the fun we had watching Ted Williams, Jackie Jensen, and Roy Sievers play baseball that afternoon. I didn't always agree with my father over the years, but I think he had the right idea that summer.

My ministry also grew more effective when I learned to take time off, not just time off from church work, but time off from all work. When I had tried to spend every moment improving myself or achieving something, I had seemed always on edge because I was forever looking beyond the present moment to a future I was trying to create or manage. I stopped doing that when Pam and I moved to Alabama in 1990. It may have had something to do with living in the Deep South, a region known for its laid-back pace, or the difference between a small town and a big city, but the main thing was the change in me: I had begun to allow myself to do nothing. As rector of St. Paul's, Daphne, I worked hard, but I worked fewer hours than in my earlier parishes. Occasionally I didn't do something I might have done, choosing instead to leave the office early to walk along the beach with Pam and enjoy a seafood supper overlooking the Gulf of Mexico. Some things in the parish didn't get done, or were done later or by someone else, and the parish seemed none the worse for it. In fact, as the world judges things, my ten years in Alabama were the most "successful" of my ministry. They were also my most relaxed, and I'm sure there's a connection.

I realized I had turned an important corner when, midway through my time at St. Paul's, I was invited to submit my name to a large parish in Atlanta that was seeking a rector. Accept a call to a church four times the size of my present one? Leave the obscurity of Daphne, Alabama, for a top job in the South's leading metropolis? Ten years

earlier, I would have said yes, but both Atlanta and I had moved —
and in opposite directions. When I first knew her, Atlanta was an
unassuming little town. She had *Gone with the Wind,* Ralph McGill,
and Coca-Cola, but that was about all. Ralph McGill was gone now,
and in his place were the Braves, the Falcons, CNN, the Olympics,
the Atlanta Symphony (actually, it *would* have been nice to live in
the same town as Yoel Levi), Lenox Square, subways, light-years of
eight-lane freeways, and an airport that threatened to consume half
the farms between Atlanta and Montgomery. Atlanta, I decided, was
a town on the go for people on the go, not for those who had learned
to value moments of doing nothing. No, thanks.

The biblical word for restful living is "sabbath." The root word is
a Hebrew verb meaning "to stop, desist." Only secondarily does the
word mean "to rest," and that rings true, for you've got to stop before
you can rest. Both body and mind must stop. When the body stops
but the mind keeps running, we lie awake, fidgeting away the early-
morning hours, exhausted as dawn approaches. *The* sabbath is the
seventh day of the week, designated as a day to cease working, to rest,
but the sabbath concept applies to shorter and longer periods of time
as well. Each day needs its sabbath moments — an early-afternoon
nap or a refreshing walk or jog. A year needs its sabbath times — like
the vacation my father would have planned. And a long career needs
sabbatical leaves, periods of several weeks or months for study and
refreshment of the spirit having no direct bearing on career tasks. In
my sabbatical leaves from St. Paul's, Daphne, I acquired a doctorate in
spirituality and traveled to Zimbabwe. While what I learned probably
enriched my ministry, the primary purpose was to nourish my soul,
not to acquire new job skills. Sometimes the best sabbatical is the one
where you do nothing. It's like a field lying fallow; it produces a better
harvest afterward, but during its fallow time, it merely rests.

There is group of Hebrew verbs variously translated as "to hope," "to trust," and "to wait." In some cases a Hebrew word can be translated with any of the three English words. The Psalms in particular abound in this:

> Tarry and await the Lord's pleasure; be strong, and he shall comfort your heart. (27:18)

> Be strong and let your heart take courage, all you who wait for the Lord. (31:24)

> Be still before the Lord and wait patiently for him. (37:7)

> And now, what is my hope? O Lord, my hope is in you. (39:8)

> I am like a green olive in the house of God; I trust in the mercy of God for ever and ever. (52:8)

> Whenever I am afraid, I will put my trust in you. (56:3)

> For God alone my soul in silence waits; from him comes my salvation. (62:1, 6)

> Let me hear of your loving-kindness in the morning, for I put my trust in you. (143:8)

> The Lord has pleasure in those who fear him, in those who await his gracious favor. (147:12)

If we would know God, we will not find him in an instant, nor will we find him by working at finding him. Our intelligence, hard work, and bright personality might accomplish some things, but sometimes they don't. If we are faithful and wise, we learn to hope, to trust, and to wait, as the psalmists say. We cannot know what the future will bring, and sometimes there isn't much we can do about it anyway, but we know that the future belongs to God. So we learn to do nothing — but to do nothing *expectantly*. That is what sabbath time is — doing nothing expectantly.

 **Silence**

"I don't talk on Sundays. I haven't in more than three years," wrote a fellow named James Otis in *The New York Times Magazine* a few years ago. Otis made his Sundays sound delectable:

> A typical Sunday starts late, at home. Sitting in the backyard, I listen to the sounds around me and often fall into daydreaming. After a nap, I usually read. Sometimes the day ends with a silent film....Silence is powerful, peaceful and simple. It's also wild and a little scary. As a participant or observer, conflict, humor, cooking, sex, exercise and violence are all very different in silence. Most of my important decisions are made on my quiet days. On Mondays, I always feel more settled and secure, hesitant, nonetheless, to join the talking world.

What a great idea! I thought. One full day each week to collect my thoughts, commune with God, or whatever. Of course, with me, it couldn't be Sunday. My paycheck would have stopped if I'd gone mum on Sundays. Maybe Thursdays. I told Pam I was considering taking a vow of silence one day a week. "Fine," she said. "Go ahead, and *I'll see if I notice the difference!*" Pam can get her point across.

There had been a time earlier in my life when silence made me squirm. I recall once in the 1970s when I had gone off for a week of what was then called "sensitivity training." We were arbitrarily divided into groups of about ten persons and put in a room. That was it. No introductions, no instructions, nothing. We had two facilitators, but they just sat there. No one knew what to do, so no one did anything. The silence lasted fifteen minutes. Finally I could stand it no longer and said, "What's our agenda?" That, I discovered, was what the facilitators had been waiting for. They knew that sooner or later someone would become so uncomfortable that he would say something, and that would elicit comments from others, and then we'd "relate" to each other. Everyone began talking about why I felt I had to have an agenda, what in my childhood had caused me to be so "task-oriented," and whether I could learn to loosen up and let my intuitive side out of the box in which I obviously kept it locked up. It was a long week.

In those days, my mind was usually full of noises — televisions and radios, cars, phones, typewriters, people in the hall outside my door, even refrigerators and air conditioners humming in the background. And children. In the absence of actual noises, my mind created noises of its own — the worries and concerns that cluttered my soul. Even when praying, I filled the silence with the noise of my words. I led public worship that way, too. The Prayer Book suggests silence at various points in the church's worship services, but rarely did I observe a period of silence. If the rubric said something like "Silence may be kept," I made sure it wouldn't be. Gradually, however, I began to learn that it is not my job to fill silent spaces with words. It's okay to let the silence just sit there. Over the years, I came not merely to tolerate silence, but to treasure it.

Others, I learned, were as uncomfortable with silence as I had once been. I asked laypersons who led prayers at the churches I served to count silently to ten, *very slowly,* wherever silence was suggested, but if they counted to ten at all, it was never slowly. Names and prayer concerns were rattled off hurriedly, and three or four seconds at most was what passed for silence. There was barely time to catch your breath. When I led the prayers myself, I sometimes allowed for a minute or more of silence, and that made people restless. More than once someone said to me afterward, "Were you all right? We were worried about you, thought maybe you'd lost your place in the service." No, it's just that I hadn't wanted to bolt through the prayers as if the whole purpose of praying was to get to the end of it. If the bidding said to pray for "the poor, the sick, the hungry, the oppressed, and those in prison," I wanted time to visualize those people in my mind as I prayed for them. You can't pray for someone you aren't thinking about. And I wanted to do more than talk to God. I also wanted to listen for God.

Silence has less to do with what we say than with what we hear. We must stop talking if we want to hear the world around us. That world includes events and relationships through which God often speaks to us, and it's especially hard to hear what God is saying to us if we're filling up the air with our own words.

Even after we've stopped talking it can be difficult to hear the voice of God, because God speaks in tones that are subtle and often ambiguous. Silence, then, isn't something we value for its own sake, but as a means to create a place where we can hear God and welcome God into our lives. God affords us what we cannot ourselves provide, and in silence we prepare ourselves to receive it.

There is an outer silence and an inner silence. Outer silence occurs when we eliminate distracting sounds from our surroundings. It is relatively easy to achieve. All you have to do is drive to some remote place, turn the car engine off, and sit there. But it's inner silence that nourishes the soul, and that's harder to find. Although inner silence can be achieved without outer silence, outer silence encourages inner silence. Inner silence is, as Thomas Merton has said, "the tuning out of that inner dialog with self that is a jumble of frivolous thoughts, worrisome cares, and negative feelings." It is, again as Merton put it, refusing to listen to "our noise, our business, our purposes, and all our fatuous statements about our purposes, our business, and our noise."

Inner silence comes slowly. It's like the silence after a train or air-plane has passed by: the noise doesn't end in an instant, but fades away. In my daily prayers, I allow several minutes of silence before reading, speaking, or doing anything with words. I do this early in the morning (before dawn is best), when both the house and my mind are still. Many people these days sit silently for twenty minutes every day, clearing their minds of everything except a focus word or phrase. This is called "centering prayer." An occasional week of silence at a monastery, under the direction of an experienced monk who sug-gests Bible passages and topics for reflection, is also helpful. One talks during such a retreat only at worship and for an hour each day with one's director. It has been during such retreats that I have heard the voice of God most deeply. Jesuit priests make a twenty-eight-day re-treat every year, and Jesus spent forty days in the wilderness alone. A few people even live their entire lives in silence. This began with the desert fathers of third-century Egypt and continues today in the contemplative monastic orders around the world.

Silent times are pleasurable for me, but the important thing about them isn't the pleasure I derive from them. It's the way I'm learning to maintain an inner center of silence even when noisy events swirl around me. Full calendars, phone calls, and to-do lists are a normal part of living. They cannot be avoided, and God wouldn't want us to avoid them if we could. The secret to serenity is not to refrain from talking one day a week. It's not even to carve out a time for silence every day, or to go off for an extended silent retreat. These things can help, but they guarantee nothing. We find real peace only when we surrender our wills to God. That always requires changes in what we do with our time and money, which is why we resist it. But once we make that act of surrender, no amount of noise will invade the quiet welling up in our souls.

Sin

I no longer talk much about sin. When the letter I wrote to a woman debating whether to have an affair was printed in the *Mobile Register*, a daily newspaper (see above, page 103), I received a note from a woman who agreed with what I had written but asked why I had not called adultery what it is — *sin.* I had not even used the word, she pointed out. But the omission was by design. It's not that I don't believe in sin — the reality of sin seems unmistakable given what human beings have done with God's world — it's that I think the word has ceased to be useful. It's been trivialized. People who eat rich desserts often say, "This is sinful!" It may be sinful, especially if it is a regular, obsessive behavior — gluttony is one of the seven deadly sins — but eating one dessert is hardly the sort of thing that lands a soul in hell.

Equating sin with sexual behavior is another way to trivialize it. To many people, especially those outside the church, the word "sin" suggests a rigid — and in their view, archaic — moral code with heavy emphasis on steering clear of sex. Sin does manifest itself in sexual wrongdoing, but it is deeper than any mere behavior. Dorothy Sayers, author of the Lord Peter Wimsey mystery stories, wrote a charming and insightful essay entitled "The Other Six Deadly Sins," addressed to a young man who, thinking sin and lust were synonymous, had said to her, "I didn't know there were seven deadly sins; please tell me the names of the other six." Sin equated with sex becomes a topic for spoofing, as in Dana Carvey's Church Lady on the television program *Saturday Night Live.* Church Lady also exuded self-righteousness, an especially sinful state of the soul to which those who speak often of sin seem singularly inclined.

Sin is also one of those words that has little meaning outside religious discourse. It's part of the church's special in-house lingo. You may hear the word in church, but you're not likely to hear it on the street, which means it doesn't relate to people's day-to-day lives. If you want to speak of sin in a way that brings people to recognize themselves as sinners, use some other word.

What is sin? It's not what you do or don't do, but a state of being. It's more like brokenness than getting broken, more like being sick than doing something that damages your health, more like alienation than behaving in a way that alienates people. You see this in Psalm 51, a classic expression of the experience of sin. The psalmist speaks of being tarnished, stained, broken, "wicked from my birth, a sinner from my mother's womb." I have heard this idea pooh-poohed. "How could an infant be guilty of sin?" people ask, as if to ridicule the very notion of infant sinfulness. Someone who cannot conceptualize the idea of rules cannot be held accountable for breaking a rule, they rightly say — but sin isn't a matter of breaking rules. If sin is a state of being, however, an infant is as suitable a candidate as anyone else.

The often misunderstood doctrine of "original sin" points to sin's pervasiveness. The world is warped by human willfulness and selfishness. Like it or not, infants are born into this world, and they are caught up in its ways long before they are capable of conscious choices. There is no escaping it. It's not as if infants had a variety of worlds to choose from and decided on a broken world over a whole world. Sin is part of what it means to be human, as much as having a heart and lungs. To be born is to become part of a web of tangled, knotted relationships, and you can't break out of it, no matter how much you'd like to. You can swear off sin until you're blue in the face, but it will still be there, surrounding you like the summer haze. Every time you take a breath, you breathe it in. Like the *Atlanta Journal,* it "covers Dixie like the dew," to say nothing of the rest of the world. And as for infants, they are the most self-centered of creatures, who, if they want something, scream and create chaos until they get it, never mind the needs and feelings of others. This is a veritable definition of what sin looks like. It's a lucky thing for infants that they're so cute, because if they weren't, no one would put up with them for a minute.

A couple came to see me several years ago concerned about something I had said in a sermon which they took to mean that I made light of sin. They wanted to know exactly what I thought of sin, and in particular, whether there were gay people in my congregation. I replied that I not only believed in sin, but thought it was awful, both because of what it is and because of its pervasiveness. We had all sorts of sinners at our church, I said, straight and gay sinners, rich and poor sinners, old and young sinners, lay and ordained sinners, in-the-closet and in-your-face sinners. Sin was, in fact, the only thing everybody at church had in common. "Sinners are the only people we've got here," I said. But we are *redeemed* sinners, I added, whom Christ loves, for whom he died, and whom he is re-creating into his likeness.

Again mentioning homosexuality, the couple asked about the woman caught in adultery in John 8. Jesus told the woman to "go and sin no more," they reminded me. Indeed, he did. His first remark, though, was to those who had condemned the woman: "Let him who is without sin cast the first stone." Jesus then told the woman to go and sin no more, but he didn't dwell on her sin — he didn't even name it. It was pretty obvious what it was, and I suppose she had already confessed it and Jesus felt it didn't require belaboring. The point of the story, as I take it, is that we should repent of our own sin as it leaks out from within us, not as we see it leaking out from other people. No finger-pointing, unless we're standing before a mirror.

One of my visitors then raised a troubling question: "If you leave it at that, what guidelines do you have? Do you just tell your children that everyone is a sinner and that everything is relative and hard to figure out?" I admitted that I struggle with that question. I said that while I once saw most things in black-and-white terms, the older I get, the more gray I see, both in the world around me and in the world within me. Nowadays, I said, for me it's usually a case of trying to distinguish between shades of gray. And yet, I am not a relativist and I do believe in absolute standards; I'm just not always sure what they are or how to apply them, especially to other people. I remember telling my visitors that I probably err more in accepting some of what God rejects than in rejecting some of what God accepts.

Except perhaps for questions of public policy, where the effects of sin can be especially blatant and destructive, I concluded early in my ministry that God probably did not want me to spend my time trying to identify and correct other people's sin. There are three reasons that I believe this: First, since sin is universal among human beings and has been for as long as anyone can remember, it's unlikely that I can eradicate it, or even make much of a dent in it. God will have to tend to that. Second, since I can't even figure out in some cases what's sinful and what isn't, I'm not the one to embark on a campaign to set everything right. And third, focusing on the sin of others deflects my attention from the only sin which, by the grace of God, I can do much about: my own.

Theology

As with so much else, C. S. Lewis understood the importance of theology. In *Mere Christianity* he writes:

> I remember once when I had been giving a talk to the R.A.F., an old, hard-bitten officer got up and said, "I've no use for all that stuff. But, mind you, I'm a religious man too. I *know* there's a God. I've *felt* him: out alone in the desert at night: the tremendous mystery. And that's just why I don't believe all your neat little dogmas and formulas about him. To anyone who's met the real thing they all seem so petty and pedantic and unreal!"
>
> Now in a sense I quite agreed with that man. I think he had probably had a real experience of God in the desert. And when he turned from that experience to the Christian creeds, I think he really was turning from something real to something less real. In the same way, if a man has once looked at the Atlantic from the beach, and then goes and looks at a map of the Atlantic, he also will be turning from something real to something less real: turning from real waves to a bit of colored paper. But here comes the point. The map is admittedly only colored paper, but there are two things you have to remember about it. In the first place, it is based on what hundreds and thousands of people have found out by sailing the real Atlantic. In that way it has behind it masses of experience just as real as the one you could have from the beach; only, while yours would be a single isolated glimpse, the map fits all those different experiences together. In the second place, if you want to go anywhere, the map is absolutely necessary. As long as you are content with walks on the beach, your own glimpses are far more fun than looking at a map. But the map is going to be more use than walks on the beach if you want to get to America.

I would add one thing. The historic creeds, as summaries of Christian belief, serve as a kind of pledge of allegiance. As a Christian, I commit myself week by week to the same defining affirmations about

God to which a hundred generations of Christians before me have committed themselves. The creeds are a song sung over two millennia. Singing with people of other times and cultures, to rhythms not our own, can be invigorating, and it's not necessary to understand what all the words mean. The creeds symbolize Christian unity through the ages and across the continents. I don't understand everything in the creeds because the language and thought forms are archaic, and I sometimes question certain statements contained in them. Some of the faithful may question every word of the creeds, and that doesn't bother me — there's nothing wrong with questioning things.

Total consensus on theology may forever elude us. The creeds are historic symbols of who we are as Christians, not straitjackets within which we must confine everyone. They are a badge Christians wear, a banner beneath which we carry on, our identifying emblem or insignia. We walk beneath that emblem, hand in hand with those who have come before us and those who will follow after us. Church doctrine defines our identity, affords us traveling companions to support us along the way, and keeps us from veering too far off the road.

Having said that, I can now say that as I've grown older, I've become less concerned about theology. I once thought that theological precision and purity were critical, and I plowed through theological books seeking to understand the key teachings of the Christian faith. The Trinity and the Atonement in particular baffled me.

Important as the creeds are as symbols of unity and continuity, I have learned to hang a bit loose. I now accept in others some beliefs (and some behaviors) that are not my own and that I once would have repudiated. Christian faith I now see as a living thing, always growing and evolving. It's fluid, or "plastic," as William Porcher DuBose said a century ago. I've changed my mind on a number of theological points over the years, and the church as a whole has changed its mind over the centuries. God calls us not so much to accept a set of doctrines as to accept his love and to return it. Besides, there is no uniformity of belief. Never has been. The creeds themselves haven't changed in nearly two millennia, but the church's understanding of what they mean is always changing. Every idea was new once. Theology thought heretical when first articulated (such as that of Paul, Aquinas, Luther, Calvin, Cranmer, and Wesley) often becomes the next generation's orthodoxy. The creeds are an indispensable theological anchor, but they do not secure uniformity of belief.

Where does theology come from, anyway? It is the product of the human mind reflecting on the experience of God. Yes, the mind is guided by the Holy Spirit, but it is not guided into a closed box. Moreover, theological statements are propositional, left-brained, intellectual. That doesn't mean they're bad, but it does mean they're derivative and secondary, not original and primary, as Lewis pointed out. The danger is that theological statements may be mistaken for the reality. Oswald Chambers put it well:

> [People] worship an intellectual creed, and you can't dispute it because it is logically correct, but it does not produce saints. It produces stalwarts and stoics but not New Testament saints, because it is based on adherence to the literal words rather than on a vital relationship to God, who is the one abiding reality. . . . It is quite possible to have an intellectual appreciation of the redemption without any experience of supernatural grace; an experience of supernatural grace comes by committing myself to a person, not to a creed or a conviction.

Thomas Merton called it our "unconscious idolatry, centered upon the illusion of a fixed idea." The idea may be true in itself, he said, but we give it "a disproportionate place in our own interior life. So it becomes an idol, drawing to itself the worship and attention and trust that we owe to God alone."

No religion or theological statement, even the Christian religion and Christian theological statements, can encompass the reality of God. The most profound theologian gains only a fleeting glimpse of God. To take Lewis's image of the man on the seashore one step further, religious believers are like people whose knowledge of the ocean is limited to a few stories about fishing and a walk along the beach. Such knowledge is accurate, but incomplete. A better understanding will incorporate the insights of others whose experiences of the ocean differ from ours and can complement and enlarge our own. This includes, I believe, adherents of other religions and of no religion. We have things to learn from them. The reality of God is as broad and as deep as the ocean. The wise believer enriches the teachings of her own religious tradition with the insights and revelations of others.

Does this negate the uniqueness and centrality of Jesus Christ? Not at all. It is merely to acknowledge that the human mind will never fully encompass nor human language express the wonders of his grace. Salvation is by grace alone. Theological beliefs (and behaviors) vary, and these differences sometimes create stress in the body of Christ. It has ever been so and will probably ever be so. But the unity of the body is threatened only when part of the body elevates its theology to the place where God alone should be enthroned. When I meet someone who confesses, "I once was lost but now am found, was blind, but now I see," I do not ask whether he believes in the Trinity. Rather, I embrace that person as my brother or sister in Christ.

Un-

I once read a book entitled *Loving, Wise, and True.* It was about the qualities desirable in a priest. The gist of the book was contained in its title, and I didn't quarrel with any of it, but I wondered why a book with that title would pertain only to the clergy. Would we not like other people to be loving, wise, and true as well? Then I thought of the fruits of the Spirit listed in Galatians 5:22. Those words were intended to describe all baptized persons, not just the clergy: love, joy, patience, kindness, generosity, faithfulness, gentleness, and self-control.

The odd thing was that when I began to reflect first on the three traits in the book title and then on the verse from Galatians, the people who came to my mind were often ones who had *not* exhibited those qualities, but rather their opposites. For some perverse reason, I seem to take more pleasure in stewing over people who are *un*loving, *un*wise, and *un*true than in celebrating those who are loving, wise, and true. In fact, I rather like that little prefix *un-*. It can be tacked onto the front of many a beautiful word to create an ugly one, and ugly words get my adrenaline pumping. So here's a list of other *un-* words that have characterized some people I've known. What I've learned from them is that I don't want to be like them.

Unripened

God knows there must be something appealing about youth, because everybody I know envies the young, and hundreds of billions of dollars are spent every year to make people look or feel younger. I don't see the point of it all. Granted, there are things about growing old that I don't look forward to, like acquiring assorted aches and pains and losing my mental capacities. But I don't mind my sagging chin and my thinning, whitish hair. They make me look — well, *wiser*. This may be an illusion. I may be as much out to lunch now as I was forty years ago, but I don't think so, and I don't want anyone who sees me to think so. Why would I want to look like an inexperienced, naive, green-behind-the-ears youth again? Thank you, but I'll keep that ripened look I see in the mirror every morning.

Unsalted

Salty language has its place (though normally not in church), and I'd rather be known as salty than bland. There have been times when I know I've come across as bland, such as when I was invited to a Super Bowl party and couldn't remember which teams were in it. At a World Series party, however, I bristle with flavor because I remember Willie Mays's catch of Vic Wertz's centerfield drive in the Polo Grounds in 1954 and Johnny Podres's two wins against the New York Yankees the next year. Most sports fans today haven't even heard of Vic Wertz and Johnny Podres. Deliver me, please, from places where my ignorance of things other people care about makes me come off as boring, and deposit me, please, where my knowledge of obscure facts makes me sparkle.

Unbruised

Sure, it's no fun to get beat up and knocked down, and it will suit me fine if it never happens to me again. I have a sufficient collection of bruises already. But I'm glad I have them because I learned more from each failure and embarrassment than from the few effortless successes that have come my way (not that there were that many). I suspect one reason God does not holler at us to warn us when we're about to blunder into something painful is that he knows that's the way people learn things, including the importance of turning to him.

Untainted

To be untainted is to be pure, free from smudges and contamination. I wouldn't want that, at least not all the time. There will be time enough for that in heaven. Moreover, the people I've known over the years who have been untainted — or more accurately, who carried on as if they were — have been insufferable prigs. Having soiled my soul over the years with my share of tawdry thoughts and behaviors, which need not be enumerated in this book, I have learned that I don't appreciate light unless I've known darkness, health unless I've known sickness, wholeness unless I've known brokenness. I suspect it's God who brings good out of all the tarnished imperfections of our lives.

Ungrammatical

Here I have a confession to make. I have a thing about dangling participles, split infinitives, and pronouns that don't agree with their antecedents. This isn't to say I *never* resort to such constructions in my own writing, but when I do I know I'm doing it and I do it for a reason. Then, when I read some other fellow's prose and find it brimming with grammatical violations, I say to myself, *What a sloppy writer!* And now for my confession: it makes me feel smugly superior to think that I can write more clearly than other people, and feeling that way is a sin.

Unhitched

Marrying the right woman thirty-six years ago is the smartest thing I ever did (though it was mostly luck, because I didn't know either her or myself well at the time, though I thought I did). Without her, I'd be a boat with neither anchor nor lighthouse. I also know that I'm hitched to hundreds of other people I've known, people with whom I have worked and prayed, laughed and cried, struggled and celebrated. I love them still and can't imagine my life without them. And I'm hitched as well to countless other baptized Christians over twenty centuries whose names I shall never know but whose prayers and fellowship hold me up. I look forward to linking arms and joining my voice with theirs some day as we stand before the one seated on a throne before a glassy sea.

Unthankful

If I had to agree to be everything on this list but one, to choose just one *un*-word to be delivered from, this would be it. On Thanksgiving Day every year, I draw up a list of things I'm thankful for — people, places, memories, tastes, colors, sounds, challenges, and my hopes for the future and the world to come. At this time in my life, I am perhaps the happiest person I know. Some, thinking of their grievances, say, "Why me, O Lord?" I say it because of my blessings — and I don't know the answer. I only know that I cannot count the things for which I am thankful. "Thank you, Lord" — and may I never forget to say it.

$\mathcal{V}$ _____ Visiting

Visiting is, traditionally, an important part of parish ministry. Early in my ministry, I had in the back of my mind the model of an ideal described in 1632 by George Herbert, whose book *The Country Parson* I had read and digested. Herbert wrote, "The country parson upon the afternoons in the weekdays takes occasion sometimes to visit in person, now one quarter of his parish, now another." By this means, Herbert felt, the parson came to know his people "most naturally as they are." I wanted to know my parishioners "most naturally as they are" and accepted Herbert's idea that regular visiting in the parish was the way to do it.

Herbert's model of ministry served me well in my first cure, St. Stephen's, Romney, a congregation of a few dozen households. Taking an afternoon or so each week, I had visited everyone within a few months. These were substantial visits, of over an hour in many cases, and I was able to return a second and third time within a year when more frequent visits were desired. I quickly came to know the people in Romney "most naturally as they are," and I loved them. When Pam and I left Romney and moved to St. John's, Charleston, where I was the assistant with primary responsibility for youth programs, I visited in homes occasionally, but another senior priest had the primary responsibility for visitation.

Then Pam and I moved to Fairmont, where we spent seven of our happiest years. We felt embraced by the people of Fairmont, both parishioners and other townspeople. As rector of Christ Church, I visited

173

every household in the parish at least once, and in most cases more than once, from three-story English Tudor mansions to house trailers up in the hollows. In time, I knew everyone, where they lived and worked and how they felt about where they lived and worked. Our children had played with their children at school and in their homes. When problems arose — loss of job, strained marriages, children in trouble — I knew of it and prayed with my parishioners about it, and because I'd sat in their living rooms or at their kitchen tables in happier days, it felt natural to be there again during a crisis time. I got to know the people of Christ Church well enough to look upon them as friends, and eventually to love them. After a few years, I felt that way about practically everybody in Fairmont. George Herbert continued to serve me well.

That was my model for ministry when I arrived at St. Peter's, Ladue, in 1982. I'd visited every household in my Romney and Fairmont parishes and it had paid off, so I'd follow the same approach in Ladue. Stupid idea! It wasn't that St. Peter's people were unfriendly or hard to love, but that there were so many of them. The active communicants at Christ Church, Fairmont, had numbered no more than 250. With some time and work, you can get to know 250 people well enough to love them — but 1,200 people? That's what I set out to do. I counted 564 households affiliated with St. Peter's when I arrived, and I resolved to see the inside of every one of those 564 living rooms. As I figured it, working forty-eight weeks each year, with two evenings and one afternoon of visiting each week, I could do fifty households a month. I'd be done with the whole thing in just over a year.

It didn't work, of course, and I should have known it wouldn't work. It was a ludicrous undertaking. I tried to visit four homes each evening, which could be done only by making advance appointments, one each for 7:00, 7:45, 8:30, and 9:15. Allowing ten minutes to drive between homes, I would spend just over half an hour with each family — and that's the way it worked at first. The first ten minutes of my visits were devoted to laying out cookies and coffee and my commenting on how tasty the refreshments were — four servings of cookies and coffee per evening. After munching and sipping for a few moments, I asked where the children went to school and where the parents worked. They asked a couple of questions about me. So I was from Kentucky, eh? They had a friend in Paducah — did I by any chance know the Hendershots from Paducah? Then we might mention something about church, probably how happy I was to be their rector and how happy they were that I was their rector. All very nice, very pleasant. But then I'd say, "Well, I've really got to be going. The Arbogasts are expecting me in ten minutes. I've sure enjoyed getting to know you all. See you in church!" If these conversations achieved anything, I don't know what it was. Time did not allow for talking about anything in depth, and I was always conscious of the ticking clock. I learned a lot of faces and names, but formed few significant relationships as a result of these visits.

And of course people didn't stay put. After less than a month of this regimen, I heard that two of my early visitations were relocating to Kansas City and Newark. How could they do this to me? I had already checked them off my list, done them, another notch in my gun belt! And then there were the new people moving in — more names when I'd hardly begun to tackle the old ones.

The main thing wrong with my visitation scheme, however, was the toll it took on me. I was never at home. With vestry meetings and other evening obligations, two evenings of visiting per week meant that I ceased to function as a husband and father. I recalled an incident from the autobiography of newscaster Dan Rather. While sitting at home one afternoon, Rather overheard his young son talking to a friend in the next room. "Is that your dad in there?" the friend asked.

"No," his son answered, "that's Dan Rather." That story sent a chill through me. Something had to change.

I junked my crazy visitation scheme after a few months. If I hadn't, I'd have become emotionally paralyzed and depressed. One parishioner, with whom I had shared all this, said to me, "I never knew why you set out to visit everybody in the first place. We're not used to that here. We don't expect it of you. When you stopped at my house that evening, I was pleased to talk with you, but I thought that wasn't the best use of your time." He was right. My new, more relaxed scheme was to visit personally only (1) those with particular needs such as the sick, the shut-ins, and the bereaved, (2) newcomers, (3) people who asked me to visit them, and (4) people with major parish responsibilities. Sometimes I recruited others to do even these visits. This proved a realistic plan, and I was able to keep it up for the most part. I also found that other people at St. Peter's were happy to be asked to share in pastoral ministry.

At about the time I went to St. Peter's, Arlin Rothauge published a splendid little booklet, "Sizing Up a Congregation," which quickly became a standard text about how congregations function. It applies to all denominations. Rothauge provided a theoretical framework that made sense of my experiences. He described four kinds of congregations, based on size. St. Stephen's, Romney, had been a "family" church in Rothauge's scheme, with fewer than 50 active members. In a family church, the pastor functions as a kind of chaplain. A "pastoral church" has 50–150 active members. Christ Church, Fairmont, had been a "program church," with an active membership of between 150 and 350. A program church's energy is in personal relationships among parishioners engaged in various tasks of ministry. The pastor's job is to know people, train leaders, delegate responsibility, coordinate everything, preach, and lead worship. St. Peter's, Ladue, was a "corporation church" (350 members or more) with an active membership approaching 1,000 people. In a church of this size, Rothauge said, the pastor knows few people well, but that doesn't matter because most people don't expect or want a close personal relationship with their pastor. He functions as a public figure and visible symbol of unity. The pastor's preaching and the conduct of worship become very important. An effective ministry depends on "sizing up" your congregation and then offering the appropriate kind of leadership

I felt liberated when I realized I didn't have to do all the visiting. But I still felt — and still feel — that visiting people is important. I once had a friend, rector of a large parish, who told me, "I don't make routine parish calls. If the people need me, they know where to find me." He was right, I think, not to make routine parish calls — his congregation was too large for that — but his remark revealed an uncaring attitude toward his parishioners, and they soon discerned it. He was courageous in the stands he took on public issues, but he split his parish, and when he eventually moved on, he left blood on the floor. I believe he would have had more support for his public stands had he cared as much about people as he cared about issues.

Visiting people is important for a theological reason as well: the incarnation of the Son of God was a divine act of visitation. He "came to visit us in great humility," as the collect for Advent I puts it. To visit people, to spend time with them in their homes and workplaces, is to identify with them, to share their lives with them. That's what God did with us. As they say in the Peace Corps, "People don't care how much you know until they know how much you care." The focus is on the relationship, not the task. That's also what parish visiting is about. It isn't important that the pastor be the chief visitor, and in large congregations it is important that the pastor *not* be the chief visitor. But a church that visits and spends time with people conveys the love of God in the way that God himself conveyed it in the person of Jesus.

 **Worldviews**

I attended several diocesan and national church conventions over the years where the air was tense and hostile. The issues varied — Prayer Books, sexuality, money, doctrine — but the feeling was the same. I was usually glad to depart such gatherings and return to my parish, where — usually — people managed to get along more amicably.

I gradually came to see that there are two ways of looking at the world, each accepted by a segment of the church, and the differences between them often surface at regional and national meetings. One group sees two armies facing off across a battleground. Everyone must enlist in one army or the other. The forces of light and truth are on one side; those of darkness and falsehood are on the other. The charge has been sounded; the battle is engaged. The second group feels the battle is already over. Both sides may now bring their wounded to the hospital of the victor for healing, where no distinction is made between victor and vanquished. Former enemies can become friends. Prejudice and misunderstanding are giving way to reconciliation and acceptance. Unity overcomes estrangement.

These two worldviews surface in other religions as well. Christianity is not the only faith community dealing with them today. But is one view of the world more consistent with the Christian gospel than the other? Which is the Christian view of the world? Both views find support in the Bible. Those who see the world as a battle in progress can quote Joshua, Judges, and Revelation. They can also quote Jesus: "I have not come to bring peace, but a sword." Those who see the world as a place where peace has been declared can quote Isaiah, 2 Corinthians, and Ephesians. And they too can quote Jesus: "Blessed are the peacemakers, for they shall be called sons of God." Both views find expression in the church's hymnody: one week we urge one another to stand up, stand up for Jesus, ye soldiers of the cross, then the next week we sing that in Christ there is no east or west, in him no south or north, but one great fellowship of love throughout the whole wide earth. Controversialists and reconcilers alike find a place within the fold of Christ.

People who view the world as a battle in progress see things in either-or, right-and-wrong categories. They stand fast for principle and are sometimes perceived as inflexible. Courage is often their greatest virtue. People who view the world as a place where peace has been declared feel that everyone is more or less good and evil, every cause more or less right and wrong. They hesitate to take a firm stand and are sometimes perceived as wishy-washy. Patience is often their greatest virtue.

Perhaps it's a matter of temperament. Some people may be temperamentally disposed to see the world in terms of conflicting opposites while others are temperamentally disposed to see it as a unified whole. This side of heaven, there's no way to know which view (if either) is the right one.

During my years as a parish priest, I occasionally joined the battle, but the older I became, the less likely I was to assume the role of Christian soldier. I came to see the world as a place where peace has been declared (though not always observed). And I like seeing things that way, because I prefer serenity to tension. The dangers for me are two: (1) I may miss out on the change and growth for which tension is often the catalyst, and (2) when a strong stand is needed, I might sit uselessly on the sidelines weighing various viewpoints. Peaceful serenity can become bland complacency.

One reason I have moved toward seeing the world as a unified whole is that, looking back over more than half a lifetime, I notice that when I took an uncompromising stand for what I viewed as God's position, I sometimes later changed my mind. Perhaps God changed his mind, too, but more likely, God had been consistent all along, and I had learned some things along the way that broadened my perspective. Hindsight is not only accurate; it's also humbling. I'm not as inclined as I once was to make grand statements about truth and falsehood. God, it seems to me, often does as well by himself as with my help. So I generally let God define and defend his position while I try to love the people he has placed in my path.

There's also the example of Jesus. He was not timid in rebuking people, but he didn't rebuke the ones we might have expected: the prostitutes, cheats, outcasts, and ne'er-do-wells. He seems to have consorted merrily with them in every town he entered. He saved his rebukes for hypocrites who felt certain they knew the truth and insisted that others follow their rules. So while a case can be made for Jesus either way, it seems to me the evidence is weightier on the side of Jesus the reconciler than of Jesus the controversialist.

And finally, those who feel peace has been declared don't have to worry about which view of the world is the right one. We acknowledge our fallibility and are not entirely surprised when events prove some favorite opinion of ours wrong. And even if we are completely wrong and the world is actually a battlefield where fighting rages, there will still be a place for us, for someone must tend the wounded.

_____ **Xenophobia**

Pam and I never thought we'd be newcomers in a church, at least not the normal kind. We would, of course, be newcomers when I accepted a call to a new parish, but lots of people would know who we were before we arrived and welcome us warmly. When I left parish ministry for a time, moved to Philadelphia, and became a newspaper editor, we began searching for a church home just as other people do when they relocate. We visited seven Episcopal churches within a few minutes' drive of our home. Not wishing to be conspicuous, I never wore my clerical collar and did not identify myself as a priest.

The experience was a revelation to me. It takes courage to walk into a church as a stranger, and real determination to form friendships (a different thing from receiving a smile and handshake at the door). At one parish, no one spoke to us, either before the service or afterward. The usher handed us a bulletin as we entered, but said nothing, and after the service, on the church lawn where refreshments had been set out, we stood silently sipping lemonade while parishioners chatted with one another a few feet away. The other six parishes were only somewhat more welcoming. A person wearing a badge bearing the word "Greeter" spoke to us as we entered, and sometimes sought us out afterward as well. In several places, the rector made a point of speaking to us (but in one parish, the rector made eye contact with us and tried to get to us, but parishioners wouldn't turn loose of him). Where there was a guest book to sign, we signed it, and in two instances we received a form letter later in the week, over the rector's signature.

These gestures notwithstanding, if you add all seven visits together, I'd call the experience depersonalizing and isolating. We felt like statues, or in some cases like unwelcome interlopers or nuisances. Parishioners might as well have formed a circle and locked arms to keep us out.

There was one exception, a small out-of-the-way parish called St. Philip's-in-the-Fields. Several laypeople greeted us warmly there, none of whom seemed to have been assigned the task. The rector, Jack Jessup, was also responsive without being pushy. On Sunday afternoon, two people we had met that morning stopped by our house with a loaf of warm bread. They didn't come in, but said they'd appreciated our visit to their church that morning and hoped we'd think of St. Philip's as we ate the bread. We did — and we joined.

The reason so many congregations behave in ways that discourage visitors from returning, I am convinced, is that they are ambivalent about growth. Virtually every church member claims to want the church to grow, but deep down, not all do. Only once in thirty years did a parishioner say to me, "I don't like all these new people. I used to know everybody here. I want a *small* church!" I am convinced, however, that many Christians agree with that man deep in their hearts. It has to do with what makes us comfortable. A small, closed society in which everyone is on a first-name basis with everyone else — and that's a good description of many small congregations — is a very comfortable place for those on the inside. When someone new shows up, the coziness of the group is threatened.

Longtime parishioners have a choice when a newcomer arrives. Their inclination, typically, is to ignore the newcomer, because people naturally want to talk to those they already know. Newcomers end up standing around holding Styrofoam cups of coffee watching other people converse, as happened to Pam and me in Philadelphia. They do not return. This behavior successfully perpetuates the comfortable group for those on the inside, which is what they want. The group gradually declines in numbers as the years pass until the remaining members finally grow depressed and look around for someone (probably the incumbent pastor) to blame for the decline. I've seen it happen just that way.

The other choice is to embrace newcomers and welcome them into the group. This behavior is uncomfortable for longtime members because it entails a risk. What if, upon striking up a conversation with the stranger, we discover we have nothing in common with her? We may embarrass ourselves by forgetting her name. The stranger may tell us to bug off or say, "What do you mean you don't know me? Don't you remember when...?" These are risks willingly undertaken by members of growing, prospering churches.

Here are some things you can do to make a newcomer feel welcome: Move to the center when someone arrives and wants to sit in your pew — having to crawl over someone who refuses to budge is a turnoff. Open your Prayer Book or hymnal to the right page and offer it to the person next to you if she seems confused, then help her when it is time to turn to another section of the book. Introduce yourself during the peace if you haven't had an opportunity to do so earlier. If the stranger seems unsure how to receive communion, say, "Come with me and let me show you what to do." Invite your new acquaintance to sign the guest book or the visitor form contained in many church pews. After church, introduce her to your friends and to the pastor. Then phone the newcomer during the week to say how happy you were to worship with her and, if possible, to invite her to join you at an event at the parish.

The last parish I served, St. Paul's, Daphne, tripled in size during my ten years there. Some people, I know, thought I was the reason, and I don't deny that the congenial match between parish and rector was part of it. I was happy and the parish was happy, and newcomers quickly sensed that. But the single most important reason for St. Paul's growth was the willingness of the people to (1) invite friends and newcomers to the community to worship with them, (2) greet newcomers at church and follow up on the relationships, and (3) open the parish leadership to others.

St. Paul's newcomer ministry was by no means perfect. We often lapsed in our efforts, and by no means did everyone who worshiped with us eventually join the parish. Moreover, a couple of longtime "pillars" of the parish eventually drifted off elsewhere, partly because (they told me this) they no longer felt needed at St. Paul's. But most parishioners were delighted to incorporate all the new members into parish life. It helps if you have a good preacher, good music, a good location, and a good children's program, but the most important thing in making a new person feel at home is the parishioners. If visitors feel that they matter and if significant relationships are formed with parishioners, they will come back — and if they don't, they won't.

$\mathcal{Y}$ _____ Youngsters

I love teaching. For most of my life I taught two or three classes of adults each week. Sometimes I used curricula available from church supply houses, but I usually designed my own curriculum.

As I have heard other teachers say, I always learned more than my students. One teaching experience in particular brought this home to me. For several weeks in 1997, I taught fourth-, fifth-, and sixth-graders, what was called the Intermediate Class. I taught them the Bible — or at least that's what I set out to do. Actually, I'm not sure they learned much about the Bible, but I learned a lot.

I should pay deep homage to Sunday school teachers. If there is a more challenging job, I don't know what it is. My first mistake was thinking I was supposed to be a nice guy, accepting everything a child said or did. But by my third Sunday, I had learned it is not out of line for a teacher to say, "My job is to talk and yours is to listen and be still. When you are to speak or walk around, I shall so inform you. Until then, make like a statue!" To my surprise, the children did as I told them — usually — but I had to tell them what I expected first. I learned to give instructions quietly, lovingly, with a sense of humor, but firmly.

I also learned that it doesn't do to reach onto the shelf, pull down a bunch of Bibles bound in black simulated leather with microscopic print, and say, "Now let's all read about the boy Samuel and how the Lord called to him one night." Most intermediate-age children, it seems, aren't keen to read anything that looks as if it comes from a century-old church archive. The next Sunday, I found another trans-lation of the Bible, with illustrations and in a vocabulary accessible to grade-school children. I enlarged the pages on the photocopier and distributed them. That worked better, though photocopied pages, un-like leather-bound Bibles, made good paper airplanes. But the children were paying some attention, or at least I was able to convince myself they were.

Once again I was reminded that most Episcopal children know almost nothing about the Bible. I had made that distressing discovery some years earlier when Pam and I volunteered to sponsor the junior and senior high youth groups at St. Philip's in Oreland, Pennsylvania. The young people in both groups, to my surprise, wanted to hear Bible stories because they said they didn't know them. Pam and I told Bible stories for an entire year, beginning with Adam and Eve and ending with the Maccabees. Today's youngsters have never heard stories I learned before kindergarten. My immediate response to this discovery was to bewail the godlessness of the modern age. Parents and church both are failing to commend the faith to the next generation, and shame on them all. But then it occurred to me that this was probably nothing new. Parents in earlier ages often had things on their minds other than teaching their children about God, and the church has rarely been overly conscientious in educating its children. So you deal with life as it comes to you, not as you wish it were or as it might have been. You do the best you can, leave the results to God, and don't walk around in a stew because of things you can't do anything about.

At first, I tried teaching my Intermediate Class as I teach adults, but that didn't work. To say to children, "What does this story mean to you?" is to elicit blank stares. The question is too abstract. Even my favorite question for adults — "Where do you see yourself in this story?" — is too abstract. Children, it seems, learn more from doing than from conceptualizing. One day we developed a skit based on Elijah in the wilderness, which seemed to engage the children, particularly when we pretended to crawl into a cave. The day we were to study the story of Jesus' presentation in the Temple, in which very old and very young people both figure prominently. I passed around a box containing questions that encouraged the children to share their feelings about growing old. I was startled to learn that I was the only one in the room who looked forward to growing old. One day we ate doughnuts and Moon Pies, an activity the spiritual significance of which I cannot now recall, but which commanded everyone's attention.

Another difference between teaching children and teaching adults is that adults usually come to church because they choose to do so. My adult classes consisted entirely of people who *wanted* to be there. Children, however, are often there because *someone else* wants them to be there.

A happy learning for me was that I like intermediate-age children. Not that I thought I didn't like them. It's just that apart from rearing my own children, I had spent most of my time with adults. In teaching the intermediate class, I discovered it's easier to remember the child who resides in my own soul and to give that child his due if I spend time with real children. Jesus said that only those who become like children will enter the kingdom of heaven, and whatever it was about children that Jesus wanted adults to emulate, we'll surely do better at becoming like them if we get to know them.

Z   Zingers

Now and then someone throws a zinger at me, says or does something that catches me so off-guard that I'm left speechless — or I should be speechless. When I've responded immediately to a zinger, without taking time to reflect on it, I've sometimes regretted it.

Once I fired the organist and choirmaster, a husband-and-wife team, who had been faithful but unimaginative members of the parish staff for twenty years. New musical leadership was needed, and a lay committee had recommended a change, but most members of the choir were devoted to the old regime and were furious with me for ousting them. On the Sunday following my announcement, four members of the tenor and bass sections threw a zinger at me by getting up from their choir stalls two minutes into my sermon, clattering out of the church, and rolling an upright piano into the chancel. They then said, in a voice for everyone to hear, "We need this for later in the service." I said not a word, more because I was stunned than because I had the good sense to remain silent.

A zinger can sting because it often contains a truth we don't want to acknowledge. There may even have been a lesson for me in the childish rudeness of the choristers who interrupted my sermon that day. Had I failed to take the time to lay the groundwork that would have minimized the fallout from my controversial decision?

A zinger I received in my Fairmont parish taught me a lesson. A young mother, whom I had not seen in church for several months, phoned to ask me to baptize her newborn child at a Sunday service.

Her parents were longtime devoted members of the parish. I called on her in her home and talked through the meaning of baptism. I concluded by saying, "I hope you will take a more active part in church life as you begin to prepare for your child's baptism. That way, your child's baptism will occur within the context of your own regular worship and the vows you take will have more meaning." I thought that was rather gentle — until she threw me a zinger: "In other words, I must live my life according to your rules in order to have my child baptized. How many Sundays must I come to church for my child to be welcome there?" She had her child baptized at another Episcopal church in the next town.

I kept up with the family. Years later, I learned that she had been struggling in a difficult marriage and that church involvement was one of the issues between her and her husband. She was trying to hold her marriage together, and church attendance on her part would have strained her already-troubled marriage. I had made assumptions about her life and the motives behind her absence from church that I had no right to make. New and unwelcome questions came to my mind: Do I have excessive control needs that damage other people? Who am I to judge whether another person is or is not a committed Christian? What can I know about the private stresses with which other people live? Is it my job to determine the validity of sacramental acts? What right have I to erect barriers to a sacrament and the divine grace it presumably bestows? Who am I to limit the work of God?

A parishioner in another parish also threw me a zinger that caused me to ask some questions. A Sunday school teacher, mother of three, and scion of an established old family of the parish came to my office to tell me she and her children were transferring to another parish. I appreciated her courage in telling of her intentions me to my face, but her announcement stung me. Then she threw her zinger at me: "Do you really think you fit in around here?" I shot back, "Yes, indeed, I feel I fit in fine around here. People have welcomed me warmly to this parish and often tell me how much they appreciate my ministry."

That's not how I really felt, although I'd been trying to convince myself it was. I remained in that parish several more years, but from that moment, I began to ask: *Do I fit in? What does it mean to fit in? Should I fit in?*

I began to see that I didn't fit in there. A gap separated my values from those of the surrounding community, my vision of the parish from that held by some of my parishioners. I felt like a woolen thread woven into a linen garment. As I reflected on the woman's zinger, I started celebrating my not fitting in. If God is always calling us to deeper and more faithful discipleship, I told myself, then a pastor who fits his environment like a hand in a glove is unlikely to see the need for change. He or she would merely reflect to the community those values with which it is already too comfortable. Everyone would enjoy the absence of conflict, but no one would be challenged to grow. Jesus, Paul, and the Old Testament prophets could have been described as misfits. Each of them stood out from their environment, in it but not of it. Priest, preacher, prophet, pastor — all those words imply a certain tension with the community, and we would be unfaithful to shy away from it.

There's truth in all that, but there's truth on the other side, too. If the gap is too large, if someone is a total misfit, she cannot minister at all. To cite an obvious example, in most parishes in this country, if a pastor possesses extraordinary gifts and insights but cannot speak English, she will have no ministry. There must be areas of congruence that bring pastor and parish together, shared experiences and perspectives, hopes and dreams. And there must be love and mutual respect. Where these are lacking, tensions will be inevitable and destructive.

We clergy must not exaggerate the degree to which we are misfits. However isolated we may feel when differences in values produce tension and the sense of not fitting in, the difference is always relative. Nearly always, the values prevalent in our parishes are largely our own values as well, and it is never a case of the parish's playing Louis XIV to our Mother Teresa. Where there is a problem, it is rarely with individuals, either ordained or lay, but with the entire social or ecclesiastical system — of which we clergy are an integral part.

In my thirty years as a parish priest, my parishioners spoke the word of the Lord to me as often as I spoke it to them — but it sometimes took a zinger for me to hear it.